A gift from
the Lander College Divisions
of Touro College
to the
Northeast Winter Regional
NER/Har Sinai Participants
5780/2020

Lander College for Women   Lander College for Men
lcw.touro.edu   lcm.touro.edu

נ"ך

A
DEEPER
LOOK

בעיון

נ"ך בעיון

A
DEEPER
LOOK

Hidden Depth and Concise Analysis
of the Prophets and Writings

ספר יהושע
SEFER YEHOSHUA

*Including an Introduction
to Studying Nach*

RABBI RAPHAEL STOHL

DISTRIBUTED BY FELDHEIM

Editing: Dr. Sheldon Stohl
Technical editing: C.D. Sklar
Page layout: E. Chachamtzedek
Cover design: M. Silverstein

ISBN 978-1-68025-406-8

DISTRIBUTED BY:
Feldheim Publishers
POB 43163 / Jerusalem, Israel
208 Airport Executive Park
Nanuet, NY 10954
www.feldheim.com

DISTRIBUTED IN EUROPE BY:
Lehmanns
+44-0-191-430-0333
info@lehmanns.co.uk
www.lehmanns.co.uk

DISTRIBUTED IN AUSTRALIA BY:
Golds World of Judaica
+613 95278775
info@golds.com.au
www.golds.com.au

Printed in Israel

From the Desk of

RABBI AHRON LOPIANSKY

Rosh HaYeshiva

YGW

Tammuz 2017

I have seen the Sefer on Yehoshua authored by Rav Raphael Stohl. The study of Tanach has been sidelined for a long time in the Torah world for many reasons, some of which the author has described in his foreword. The result is that a ben Torah who is attempting to study Tanach on his own will either find works that offer a myriad of pirushim on each point but no comprehensive thematic overview; or works that give thematic and structural overviews, but seem to be the product of the authors sense of things, with no basis in Chazal or Rishonim. This presents no small dilemma for the ben Torah seeking to study Tanach.

Rabbi Stohl has written a small but significant pirush on Yehoshua that bridges this gap. It is thematic in nature, and looks at the big picture, while finding his source in Chazal and other works of the great teachers.

It is a very important sefer, and hopefully it will mark the beginning of a genre of such works both by the author and by others.

Ahron Shraga Lopiansky

Tiferes Gedaliah- Yeshiva of Greater Washington

RABBI SHIMON KRASNER
407 YESHIVA LANE #1B
BALTIMORE, MARYLAND 21208

שמעון קרסנר
מח"ס נחלת שמעון על ספרי נ"ך
באלטימאר, מד.

י"ח אדר תשע"ח

I have known Rabbi Raphael Stohl for many years. He is a young accomplished *talmid chacham* who has taught many *talmidim* over the years.

I have read much of his new book, *Nach B'Iyun* on *Sefer Yehoshua*, and I enjoyed it very much. His introduction to the study of *Nach* is especially interesting and informative.

Although the book is small in size, it is big in content. Rather than presenting a *posuk* by *posuk* explanation of *Sefer Yehoshua*, he focuses on presenting a concise and in-depth analysis of the main points of each chapter, so that the reader can easily grasp and appreciate what the *Navi* is trying to convey. His extensive notes provide additional analysis and excellent references so that one can delve into *Sefer Yehoshua* at an even higher level.

This is an important work and I feel confident that the reader will derive much benefit from it.

I wish the author much *hatzlacha* from this book and future books that he wishes to publish. May he have continued success with all his *avodas hakodesh*.

שמעון קרסנר

Approbation from

Rabbi Michael Rosensweig *shlita*

Rosh Yeshivah and Rosh Kollel
Yeshivas Rabbeinu Yitzchak Elchanan

Rabbi Raphael Stohl, a young תלמיד חכם who was a diligent member of our Kollel Elyon, has authored a sefer on Sefer Yehoshua that identifies, elaborates and illuminates the primary hashkafic motifs in the Sefer. The work examines the central topics of the Sefer in a thematic manner (as סוגיות), providing important context, perspective, analysis, and insight on matters that are broadly of vital interest and importance to עובדי ה' of all generations. His treatment effectively reinforces the axiomatic principle of Tanach's absolute and pervasive relevance.

The mechaber makes extensive use of a wide range of traditional מקורות – Chazal, Rishonim, Gedolei Achronim, Parshanim – alongside the works of more contemporary talmidei chachomim, as he grapples with the issues engendered by a serious engagement with the text of the Navi. This approach effectively demonstrates both the rich diversity of views within our mesorah, as well as the cohesive, unifying principles that emerge from the total analysis of these סוגיות. By both juxtaposing and integrating, Rabbi Stohl develops many important specific insights and engages the topics in an intellectually and religiously sophisticated fashion.

It is evident throughout that the author's methodological approach (presented in the first chapter) is fueled by אהבת התורה, a sense of humility, a feeling of wonderment about the depth and grandeur of Torah, and especially a deep reverence – יראת שמים – regarding both the topics and their traditional treatment. It is a work that truly reflects that יראתו קודמת לחכמתו, notwithstanding considerable חכמה.

I am pleased to recommend the sefer, a felicitous meld of chidush and hemshech as an important contribution to thematic limud haTanach. I look forward to Rabbi Stohl's future contributions. יה"ר שילך מחיל אל חיל בלימוד התורה ובעבודת השם, ושיפוצו מעיינותיו חוצה להגדיל תורה ולהאדירה

בברכת התורה
א' *[signature]* ריג נ ץ ר ת"ו
הרב מיכאל רוזנצווייג

ראש ישיבה וראש כולל

ישיבת רבינו יצחק אלחנן

שמואל קמנצקי
Rabbi S. Kamenetsky

2018 Upland Way
Philadelphia, PA 19131

Home: 215-473-2798
Study: 215-473-1212

This approbation was given to the author for a previous work.

Rabbi Hershel Schachter
24 Bennett Avenue
New York, New York 10033
(212) 795-0630

הרב ה.צ. שכטר
ראש ישיבה ורם כולל
ישיבת רבינו יצחק אלחנן

אמרי דעת

אל מורי הישיב אלה דברים... הרמחל
הרית הצעיר הר' ... שלי' (בי"ה)
כתב ספר ... שם של עם ... ... על
כתב וספר ... ... אמרי ... הספר ... ורביים
מאלו מלי הדברות ... ... התשובות ...
... ספר ... ... מוברים הראשונים פס,
הכרתי ... אל ... ... הו"ל
... הרבה ... סיוון אשר ... ...
... אלול ... אלא ... ... מכ"ע
... הספר ... ... אל
ויהי רצון ... הרב ... ...
... הי' ... ... הראשונים ... אותו ... ...
... והיה ... אמר הרבה ... ...
הברכה והתחבה ... ...
... ...

ה.צ. שכטר

This approbation was given to the author for a previous work.

אשר זעליג וייס
כנן 8
פעיה"ק ירושלם ת"ו

בס"ד

התאריך _____

[handwritten text]

הן ראיתי את הספר החשוב והיקר תורת הכבוד על המצוות
השונות שבהן נצטווינו, איש את רבותיו, אביו ואמו, שבט
הכהנים וכו'. סוגיא זו עמוקה ורחבה עד למאוד, וכמדומני
שעדיין לא ראיתי חיבור המקיף ענין זה מכל צדדיו.

על כן אמרתי בואו ונחזיק טובה למחבר ספר נפלא זה,
האברך המופלא הרה"ג ר' רפאל סטוהל שליט"א, מרביץ
תורה ומזכה הרבים, שמקום הניחו לו מן השמים.

הספר מצטיין בבהירות, חכו ממתקים וכולו מחמדים, דברים
ערבים בהלכה ובאגדה, ובטוחני שרבים יאותו לאורו.

ברכתי למחבר שליט"א, שיזכה תמיד להגדיל תורה
ולהאדירה, בשמחה שלוה ונחת.

This approbation was given to the author for a previous work.

Contents

Preface

THE TORAH REFERS TO Yehoshua as a "lad who never left the tent [of wisdom]" (*Shemos* 33:11 — יהושע בן נון נער לא ימיש מתוך האהל). Rashi (*Avos* 1:1) explains that Yehoshua displayed utter disregard for the physical, engulfing himself wholly in the study of Torah. From his youth, he figuratively "sacrificed himself in the tents of wisdom" (ממית עצמו מנעוריו באהלי החכמה).

The Ibn Ezra notes that Yehoshua was fifty-six years of age at the time, already having lived over half of his life. And yet, the Torah refers to him as a "lad"![1] R. Moshe Shapira *zt"l* explains (lecture on *Parashas Zachor* 5748, as understood by one of his students) that the word "*na'ar*" (נער; lad) is associated with the Hebrew word "*lena'er*" (לנער), meaning "to shake." The word implies constant motion — a "*na'ar*" is always moving, searching for new teachings and experiences. Yehoshua, even after having lived more than half of his life, was still characterized by constant movement and desire for growth.

Yehoshua's determination to develop and progress was most clearly apparent in the realm of Torah study. R. Shapira notes that the concept of "not leaving" (לא ימיש) appears twice in regards to Yehoshua's Torah study — first, when Yehoshua is originally called a

---

1. See, however, the Ramban's response to the Ibn Ezra's comment. See also *Sha'arei Aharon* (*Shemos* 33:11) who points out that Rashi (*Sefer Shoftim* 11:26) may understand that Yehoshua was only forty-two.

"lad" (ibid.), and later in his life when Hashem impels him to engage constantly in Torah study and to never allow the Torah "to leave his mouth" (*Yehoshua* 1:8 — לא ימוש ספר התורה הזה מפיך, והגית בו יומם ולילה).

Yehoshua thus serves as a model for all serious students of Torah. He illustrates that regardless of one's age, and irrespective of the myriad responsibilities that one may have (Yehoshua was the leader of the entire Jewish nation!), the importance of Torah study must remain paramount. It needs to be constantly and consistently afforded significant time and effort.[2]

From the depths of my heart, I thank Hashem for affording me, for so many years, the distinct privilege of focusing primarily on Torah study. I am profoundly grateful for the opportunity to publish my thoughts on *Sefer Yehoshua* and to internalize its ageless lessons and wisdom. I hope and pray that Hashem continues assisting me in upholding the extraordinary responsibility of learning Torah and in trying to follow Yehoshua's remarkable example of leading a life of constant growth in the service of our Creator.

This publication is particularly meaningful to me. When I was a student in yeshivah and during my early years in *kollel*, I recognized my ignorance of *Tanach* and dreamed of one day being afforded the chance to study *Tanach* properly. When my eldest sons turned, successively, five years of age, I began learning *Nach* with each of them before bedtime, a study which provided me with a decent grasp of the basic stories and a thirst to find answers to the many questions left unanswered. A few years later, the Almighty

---

2. The Netziv (*Ha'Amek Davar, Shemos* 33:11) makes a similar point, adding that it is particularly incumbent upon full-time students to remain engrossed in Torah learning and not involve themselves in other activities (even *mitzvos*) unless absolutely necessary.

afforded me the opportunity to join the Hollywood (Florida) Community Kollel and to organize a local *Nach Chaburah*, a weekly/bi-weekly gathering of a number of community members to study the timeless teachings of the Prophets. Leading this learning group forced me to study *Nach* in depth in preparation for each *shiur* (class). The *chaburah* compelled me to explore avenues of Torah thought with which I had been previously unfamiliar (and sometimes even completely unaware), which in turn whetted my appetite to understand even more of God's great Torah. As an older friend/mentor once quipped: when it comes to the study of *Nach*, it often helps to "teach in order to learn" (ללמד על מנת ללמוד).

I sincerely thank all those who took from their time to join our *chaburah* over the years. This publication is due to *your* efforts and thirst for Torah! May Hashem provide us (and all our brethren throughout the world) with continued passion for Torah learning and allow us to remain forever grounded in the hallowed "tents of wisdom."

Acknowledgments

I EXPRESS BOUNDLESS GRATITUDE TO Hashem for blessing our warm and welcoming community in Hollywood, Florida, with the Hollywood Community Kollel. Since it opened nearly six years ago, the *kollel*, under the guidance of the *Rosh Kollel*, **Rav Moshe Baruch Parnes** *shlita*, has served as a bastion of Torah learning in our already thriving Torah community. We have been privileged to immerse ourselves in Torah study, to learn Torah with hundreds of community members on a daily and nightly basis, and to show the world the unmitigated splendor of Torah life. It is my sincere hope and prayer that Hashem continues to provide the community (along with the entire world) the opportunity to delve deeply into His holy Torah and follow His impeccable ways.

Thank you to all those who helped me reach this juncture in general and who assisted me with this publication in particular. As mentioned above, this work was inspired by a group of wonderful members of our community in Hollywood, Florida, who joined me on a weekly/bi-weekly basis to learn *Nach*. Ultimately, this work is due to their efforts and their desire to learn.

To single out just a few of the many who participated: I thank **Dr. Avi Baitner, Dr. Yitzchak Kravetz,** and **Dr. David Lasko** for their impressive consistency of attendance and support; **Mr. Yossi Mizrachi** for encouraging me (over five years ago) to assemble this *chaburah*; **Mr. Yitz Taub** for showing great interest and for tacitly inspiring me to continue even when doing so became difficult; **Mr.**

Chaim Hirsch for similar encouragement and enthusiasm. Among the numerous others who joined over the years, I want to list a number of people who participated for significant stretches of time: **Rabbi Ranan Amster; Dr. Eli Berman; Joey Betesh; Hillel Cooperman; Dr. Jonathan Dobkowski; Avi Frier; Steven Jacoby; Mark Kogan; Joel Kornbluth; Mrs. Meirav Kravetz; Josh Levine; Dr. Jonathan Mazurek; Steven Newman; Dr. Lorry Rubenstein; Uri Rubin; Dr. Abe Ruttenberg; Rabbi Howard Seif; Mathew Silverman; Jeff Simon; Ezra Splaver; Dr. Oren Stier; Dr. and Mrs. Noah and Shira Turk; Shaya Weinstein; Ari Zeltzer; Rami Zvida.** I also thank **Mrs. Lisa Baratz** for her infectious enthusiasm for *Tanach* study and for her eye-opening questions and remarks.

With a profound sense of both love and respect, I thank my *rabbeim* (those who taught me personally and those whom I know through their *sefarim*), teachers, mentors, *chavrusas*, friends, and students for all of their teaching, help, and guidance over the years.[1]

I specifically thank my *Rebbe muvhak*, **Rav Moshe Stav** *shlita*, and, *l'havdil bein chaim l'chaim*, my Rebbe and mentor, the late **Rav Dovid Landesman** *zt"l*, who molded my mind and character during my most formative years, and whose examples I constantly strive to follow in all of my learning and teaching. I also single out my Rebbe, **Rav Mendel Blachman** *shlita*, and my Rebbe, *chavrusa*, and dear friend, **Rav Chaim Packer** *shlita*, for further opening my eyes to new worlds of Jewish thought at various stages of my life. I similarly thank my dear friend and mentor, **Rav Netanel Wiederblank** *shlita*, for all his assistance and time (in person and from afar) in working through matters of Torah and Jewish philosophy.

---

1. I elaborate on the unique gift that each person bestowed upon me and the honor that each individual deserves in the *"Shalmei Todah"* section of my recent *sefer, Toras HaKavod.* The reader is encouraged to read those pages.

I extend tremendous appreciation to the numerous *rabbanim* who took time from their extremely busy schedules to read this publication and contribute comments and advice. It is a great honor to have had **Rav Ahron Lopiansky** *shlita* review my work and write a letter of commendation. Over the past year and a half, Hashem has blessed me with the opportunity to "sit in his tent" (mostly through communication from afar and through listening to his *shiurim* on an almost-daily basis). He has helped shape my mind and soul, and his Torah is extant in much of my learning and teaching. I further thank my Rebbe, **Rav Michael Rosensweig** *shlita*, for generously contributing an approbation to this publication, for years of caring instruction, and for broadening my mind with his breadth of knowledge and remarkable organization of thought. I am uniquely grateful to **Rav Shimon Krasner** *shlita*, not only for contributing a letter of commendation for this publication, but also for his fabulous set of *sefarim* on *Nach* (*Nachalas Shimon*). As apparent from the numerous citations throughout this publication, I use his works on a regular basis and have grown considerably from his Torah. I give special thanks to **Rav Yaakov Krause** *shlita*, the *mara d'asra* of Young Israel of Hancock Park in Los Angeles, California, and my family's Rav ever since I was a little boy. His help with the writing of this publication has been indispensable, as has been his assistance in many other facets of my (and my family's) religious growth. And, finally, I thank **Rav Yisroel Reisman** *shlita* for his diligent and detailed critique of earlier drafts of this publication. Rav Reisman, whose *shiurim* and *sefarim* I have enjoyed for years, took the time to scrutinize much of my writing, page by page. His forthright, instructive comments displayed incredible patience, clarity, and wisdom. It is truly an honor and privilege to have been the recipient of his personal guidance.

From the bottom of my heart, I thank my dear friend, **Mr. Jon Lasko** for his sincere love and care and for his remarkable support of Torah. May Hashem bless him and his entire family with wondrous success in both worldly and spiritual pursuits. I similarly thank all the sponsors of this publication; may Hashem repay them manifold for their generosity and support.

I am forever grateful to my dear friend, **Mr. Norman Ginsparg,** whose sage advice has greatly assisted my growth and my handling of a number of challenges in recent years. Additionally, through his tenacity and thirst for truth, Norman has helped me hone several ideas included in this work. I also thank my friend, **Noah Lasko,** for his love of learning and for his notable consistency. His desire has forced me to constantly work hard to learn, prepare, and produce. May he and his family continue to grow in Torah and *yiras Shamayim.*

I thank **Mrs. Shalva Muschel** for kindly reading and editing an earlier draft of this work and **Rabbi Eli Muschel** for his technical assistance and for acting as my liaison in New York. I further thank **Rabbi Yosef Weinstock** and **Mrs. Elaine Braun** of the Young Israel of Hollywood-Ft. Lauderdale for their care and technical support, **Mr. Ethan Berner** for his patience and assistance as we hammered out various issues of design and beyond, **Mr. Michael Chesel** for his love and care for the community (and for Klal Yisrael at large) and for his help with some technical aspects of my publications, and **Mrs. Chana Devorah Sklar, Mrs. Eden Chachamtzedek, Mr. Michael Silverstein,** and **Rabbi David Kahn** of Feldheim Publishers for their fabulous work in editing, typesetting, and design.

My deepest appreciation goes out to my dear brother, mentor, and friend, **Dr. Sheldon (Shelly) Stohl.** His character has forever served as an example that I constantly strive to emulate, and his honesty and intellectual acumen continue to help me formulate ideas of all types. Most recently, he worked tirelessly to sharpen and refine my thoughts on *Sefer Yehoshua* and to edit (and re-edit, and re-re-edit!) this entire publication.

It goes without saying that I could not have written this work, nor accomplished anything else in life, without the constant love, care, and guidance of my parents, **Dr. and Mrs. William and Avivya Stohl**. I also thank my father for assisting me greatly in editing this work, and, specifically, for his grammatical and idiomatic expertise. May Hashem bless my parents with continued health and youthfulness, and may He grant them *nachas* from all their children, grandchildren, and beyond.

I similarly thank Hashem for our entire wonderful family. My parents-in-law, **Mr. and Mrs. Fred and Clarisse Schlesinger** shower us and all members of our family with love and concern. My siblings and siblings-in-law, too, are always happy to lovingly assist in any way feasible.

And finally, I sing endless praise to the Almighty for partnering me with my wife, a true *eishes chayil*, Malki. This publication would never have been possible if not for her constant care for our children, her willingness to relinquish her own needs for others and for lofty causes, and her uncanny ability to juggle tens (if not hundreds) of responsibilities simultaneously and seamlessly. May she merit to reap and enjoy the fruits of her labor — to experience great *nachas* from our children and from all that she provides me, our family, our community, and the world.

INTRODUCTION TO
STUDYING
NACH

The Challenges of Studying *Nach*

A Glance at History and Its Implications Today

T HE IMPORTANCE OF LEARNING *Nach* (*Nevi'im* and *Kesu-vim*) is well known. The Gemara (*Megillah* 14a) states that the teachings and stories recorded by our prophets are instructive for all generations. In addition to the many *halachos* and examples of proper conduct that are gleaned from the directives of the Prophets, studying *Nach* provides us with a broad outlook of Torah values and how they should be applied.[1] Exposure to the depth of *Nach* also enhances one's

---

1. R. Yosef Breuer *zt"l* (in his essay, "Our Prophets Speak to Us," printed in *Collected Writings of R. Samson Raphael Hirsch*, vol. IV, pp. xv–xxi) elaborates upon this point:

> Let us read our Prophets if we wish to comprehend ourselves as Jews, with all the obligations which this noble title entails for us... Let us obtain clarity from our Prophets regarding that which fully characterizes the Jewish national concept: *Am Hashem* (the Nation of God)... Our Prophets never tire of defining and outlining the role of Eretz Yisrael, so that we may be able to distinguish it from the other lands in the world... Let us read our Prophets if we are to perceive the meaning of *Galus* (Exile), experience *Geulah* (Redemption), and fulfill the conditions which lead to *Geulah*...

love for Hashem and His Torah.[2] Rashi (*Shemos* 31:18; based on *Tanchuma, Ki Sisa* #16) comments that "a *talmid chachom* needs to be an expert in the twenty-four books [of *Tanach* (the five books of the Torah, eight books of *Nevi'im*, and eleven[3] books of *Kesuvim*)]." The Rambam (*Hilchos Talmud Torah* 1:11–12) further writes that only after one has attained a good grasp of *Tanach* should he focus the vast majority of his study time on Gemara. *Chazal* (*Avos* 5:21; *Kiddushin* 30a) therefore encourage teaching *Tanach* to young students.[4]

While the study of the Chumash — the first five books of *Tanach* — is familiar to most students of Torah, many people find it challenging to learn *Nevi'im* and *Kesuvim* (*Nach*). A cursory read of *Nach* often leaves the reader with more questions than answers and with a somewhat distorted picture of our rich history and

---

Prophets teach us to understand Israel's historic position always in the context of the great world historic events and developments... All this we glean from the words of our Prophets; it is Torah which we read *with them*... He who reads Prophets as they should be read receives eternally sacred messages from their mouths: This is how we, the Prophets, experienced Torah. This is what Torah means to us; what does it mean to you?

2. The Rambam (*Hilchos Teshuvah* 10:6; *Sefer HaMitzvos*, Positive Mitzvah 3) stresses that learning Torah inspires a more intense love of God. In the words of R. Ahron Lopiansky *shlita* (introduction to his *sefer, Time Pieces*, p. 27): "Torah, especially *aggadeta*, enriches and enlivens a person with *da'as Elokim* (Godly knowledge); it perforce produces *ahavas Hashem* (love of God)." *Tanach*, the corpus of Hashem's most direct words, certainly has the ability to further one's appreciation for, and love of, the Almighty and His infinite wisdom.

3. *Ezra* and *Nechemiah* were originally considered one *sefer* and were later split into two *sefarim*. See *Mishbetzos Zahav* (*Ezra, Nechemiah*, pp. 4–6, 204–5), who offers fascinating reasons for this phenomenon.

4. Although Rashi (*Kiddushin* ad loc.) understands that a father is obligated to teach his child only Chumash, the vast majority of halachic authorities, including the *Shulchan Aruch*, rule that a father is obligated to ensure that his son learns the entire *Tanach* (see *Shulchan Aruch, Yoreh De'ah* 245:6; *Beiur HaGra* ad loc.; see also *Pesakim U'Teshuvos* ad loc. 245:17).

great leaders. To gain a proper understanding of *Nach*, one needs to invest significant time and effort. The famed Mashgiach, R. Shlomo Wolbe *zt"l*, records a similar insight (in a letter of approbation to *sefer Mishbetzos Zahav* on *Sefer Yehoshua*):[i]

> My teacher and Rebbe, HaGaon R. Yosef Breuer *zt"l*, Rosh Yeshivas Frankfurt and grandson of R. Shimshon Raphael Hirsch *zt"l*, used to say that the *Nevi'im Rishonim* (Early Prophets) can be learned only by young children or great Torah scholars, for "regular people" (*beinonim*) are unable to grasp all of the difficult ideas that are found there.[5]

Therefore, many yeshivah curriculums today (post-elementary school and onward) do not focus much on the study of *Nach*.[6] The educational heads of these *yeshivos* feel that focusing on *Nach* would detract from the time and emphasis required for adequate study of Chumash, Mishnah, Gemara, and Halachah, which are most essential in a student's formative years.

This sentiment is not new. *Chazal* instruct that Gemara should constitute a student's key focus.[7] Like many educators today, a

---

5. R. Wolbe expresses similar sentiments in *Alei Shur* (vol. 2, p. 118). He adds that Torah scholars have the unique opportunity to understand *Nach* based on their knowledge of *Chazal's* explanations, but others who do not have such background in Gemara etc. are prone to confuse issues ("עלולים לעוות הבנת הדברים"). For yet another similar statement of R. Wolbe, see his approbation to R. Yitzchak Levi's *Parshiyos B'Sifrei HaNevi'im* on *Sefer Yehoshua* where he extols the author for composing a work that could assist even non-scholars in the study of *Nach*.

6. Admittedly, there are, in this regard, significant differences between schools in Eretz Yisrael and schools in America.

7. See, for example, *Bava Metzia* (bottom of 33a) and *Berachos* (28b, with *Rashi* s.v. ההגיון) that stress the importance of learning Gemara over *Tanach*. See also *Tosafos* (*Kiddushin* 30a s.v. לא), who record the prevalent custom of focusing solely on Gemara and learning only those parts of *Tanach* that are quoted by the Gemara. It seems that even some great *talmidei chachomim* lacked a strong grasp of *Tanach* (see *Bava Kama* top of 55a; *Tosafos, Bava Basra* top of 113a) and that this deficiency did not disqualify them as Torah scholars (see *Rashash, Bava Basra*

number of *Rishonim* and early *Acharonim* maintained that it is exceedingly difficult for most students during our long, treacherous exile to focus on both Gemara and *Tanach*.[8]

But this phenomenon need not deter people from delving into *Nach* as adults. Indeed, numerous contemporary Torah leaders advocate the study of *Nach*. R. Zev Leff *shlita* (Foreword to *Journey Through Nach*) is particularly encouraging, noting that many concerns that prevailed in previous eras no longer apply:

It would seem that learning and mastering the *Tanach*, the very basis of all Torah, would be an understood necessity for every Jew. Surely a *ben Torah* or *talmid chachom* could not be considered such if he was ignorant of the very foundation of all

---

8a). Quite the contrary, people who were well versed in *Tanach* but not in Gemara and Halachah were not held in high esteem (see the article, *HaMikra* etc., cited in the following footnote). Similarly, the Rashbam (*Bereishis* 37:2) writes that it was the spiritual eminence ("חסידותם") of earlier generations that brought them to focus mainly on halachic derivations and other aspects of the Oral Torah and to spend less energy on the "simple meaning of the text." [R. Yehudah Cooperman *zt"l* (*Peshuto shel Mikra*, vol. 3 — *Hashlamos*, p. 339) points out that the Rashbam makes similar comments in a number of other places as well: in his introduction to *Parashas Mishpatim*; *Vayikra* 13:2; beginning of *Parashas Bereishis*.]

A number of commentators note, however, that some *talmidei chachomim* focused mainly on *aggadah* and *Tanach* (see *Kol Sifrei Maharatz Chayes*, vol. 1, p. 317, s.v. אכן). Yet, it is likely that even those Torah scholars utilized their foundational years to study matters of halachah. Only after honing their minds and grasping the intricate laws of the Torah did they spend the majority of their time on *aggadah* (see *Rambam, Hilchos Yesodei HaTorah* 4:13).

8. For a number of citations, see Prof. Mordechai Breuer's article, *HaMikra BaTochnit HaLimudim shel HaYeshivah* (published in *Mechkarim BaMikra U'VaChinuch*, edited by Prof. Dov Rappel, pp. 233–4).

It should be noted, however, that all the above notwithstanding, numerous *Rishonim* and *Acharonim* strongly encouraged students to study *Tanach* (see footnote 4 above; see also *Abarbanel, Nachalas Avos, Avos* end of ch. 5). Interestingly, some scholars (see Prof. Breuer, ibid.) point to differences in custom in this regard between Ashkenazic and Sephardic communities. See also R. Eliyahu Krakowski's article, "Why Isn't *Tanach* Studied More?" (*Jewish Action*, Winter 2018).

learning. However, as a reaction to the *Maskilim* (those influenced by the secular "Enlightenment") who used the learning of *Tanach* to the exclusion of *Torah She'be'al Peh* (the Oral Torah), and distorted how it should be learned — to further their agenda to obliterate Torah and *yiras Shamayim* (fear of Heaven) from Klal Yisrael, the learning of *Tanach* was de-emphasized in the yeshivah world[9] ... *Baruch Hashem*, this aspect of *Haskalah*, for the most part, has passed from the world... Hence, the basic learning and knowledge of *Tanach* is something every Jew should acquire. Since this learning has been neglected for so long by the masses, any program that encourages making *Tanach* a part of one's learning and facilitates one's mastery of it is a welcome and important development.[10]

---

9. Some scholars suggest that Rabbinic reservations with the study of *Tanach* during the *Haskalah* era paralleled the Rabbinic position in the Middle Ages. At that time, a number of *Rishonim* and early *Acharonim* were apprehensive about *Tanach* study (in particular periods and locations) out of fear that students of *Tanach* would succumb to the influences of Christian Bible studies and/or various sects of reformers. (See the article cited above; see also Prof. Breuer's article, *Min'u B'neichem min HaHigayon*, p. 248, printed in *Michtam L'David*, edited by Y. Gilat and E. Stern.)

10. R. Leff's assessment that the concerns voiced by Torah leaders of previous generations regarding the study of *Tanach* no longer apply, as well as his consequent support for *Tanach* study, were apparently shared by R. Yaakov Kamenetsky *zt"l* (see R. Yisroel Reisman's *Pathways of the Prophets*, p. 362) and by the late Satmar Rebbe, R. Yoel Teitelbaum *zt"l* (see *Kovetz Beis Va'ad LaChachomim*, *Av* 5769, p. 329, fn. 40). See also the approbations to *The Navi Journey* (by R. Ilan Ginian, *Sefer Shoftim*) for a number of other contemporary Torah leaders who encourage students today to learn *Nach*. R. Shmuel Wosner *zt"l* (*Shevet HaLevi*, vol. 8, #207) similarly writes that it is obvious that one must know, at least, the basics of *Tanach*, pointing out that *talmidei chachomim* throughout the generations learned *Tanach*. He notes, however, that some Torah leaders hid their knowledge of *Tanach* lest they encourage the growing *Haskalah* movement. R. Eliyahu Meir Bloch *zt"l* (in a letter published in the 1969 ed. of *Mitzvos HaShalom*, p. 607) adds that some people continue to discourage learning *Tanach* in order to remain distanced from other modern threats, but he disagrees with this sentiment and feels that people should indeed engage in *Tanach* study. It should be further noted that

Yet, widespread and longstanding neglect of *Tanach* has, for many, rendered its study a daunting and intimidating task. R. Avraham Yitzchak Sorotzkin *shlita* (introduction to *Rinas Yitzchak* on *Sefer Yehoshua*), who authored nine volumes covering all of *Nach*, offers the following words of inspiration:[ii]

> Since my youth, I have been troubled by my limited capacity to understand even the simple interpretation of [Biblical] texts. In particular, I have found challenging the study of *Nach*, as there is a dearth of adequate available teaching and direction, and there is a lack of tradition as to how to study it, as but few delve into it. I was hungry and my soul craved to know and attain it — I studied ravenously for many years, and blessed be the Creator and praised be the Maker, for after I reviewed the *Megillos* time and again, I began to taste its [i.e., the Torah's] sweet nectar, and a window opened before me to its understanding. And I began to notice success in my studies, and through the years I toiled and succeeded... And although [a true understanding] yet eludes me, I have nonetheless seen blessing and Divine assistance accompany my labor.

The purpose of this publication is to provide a degree of depth to the infinitely profound chapters of *Nach* and to offer some answers to many of the difficult questions that can (and often should) bother the reader. My hope is that this endeavor will encourage more people to learn the works of our saintly *Nevi'im* (Prophets), even if only in a "*beki'us,*" quick-paced style.

R. Shimshon Raphael Hirsch *zt"l* (*The Nineteen Letters*, pp. 293–4, fn. 10) encouraged the study of *Tanach* even in an era during which Torah leaders viewed the *Haskalah* movement as a clear threat. He stressed, however, that *Tanach* be taught properly, in accordance with age-old tradition. (All of the above notwithstanding, there may still be some Chassidim who are advised to learn *Tanach* only as part of their study of *Torah She'be'al Peh.*)

It should be emphasized that aside from the personal obligation incumbent upon each individual to learn and grasp as much Torah as he can, studying *Nach* also provides a wonderful opportunity to learn and spend quality time with one's children. Although schools often do not have the time to afford *Nach* its due focus (as described above), parents can nonetheless learn *Nach* with their children at home. Relaying the stories of *Nach* to one's children (before bedtime, etc.) can serve as a priceless bonding experience between parent and child. Children love hearing the stories of *Tanach*, and they cherish such moments spent with their parents. There is also no better way to impart our rich *mesorah* (tradition) to our children. To help, there are some very fine children's books written on *Nach*, with pictures and wording designed for children. Titles include (not to the exclusion of any others) *Know Navi*, by R. Yaakov Hopkowitz, and *The Little Midrash Says*, by R. Moshe Weissman.

It is likewise important to note that even though *yeshivos* do not often formally teach *Nach*, many great educators encourage yeshivah students to dedicate a small amount of time each day/week to study *Nach* on their own. See, for example, the advice of R. Shlomo Wolbe *zt"l* (*Alei Shur*, vol. 2, p. 118)[iii] and R. Moshe Mordechai Shulsinger *zt"l* (*Peninei Rabbeinu HaAvi Ezri*, p. 164).[iv]

Aside from the works of the classic commentators, a number of very good books and *sefarim* can help guide those interested in delving further into *Nach*. To name a few (not to the exclusion of all other good books and *sefarim* that one may find): *Mishbetzos Zahav* (Hebrew) by R. Shabsi Weiss provides remarkable insights on *Nach, pasuk* by *pasuk*; *Nachalas Shimon* (Hebrew) by R. Shimon Krasner delves into many of the halachic issues that pertain to the various stories of *Nach*; *Torah She'Be'al Peh* (Hebrew) by R. Menachem Stern gathers many (if not most) of the relevant passages of *Chazal* on each *pasuk* of *Nach*; *Journey Through Nach* (English) by R. Daniel Fine and Chaim Golker provides helpful summaries of the text, *perek* by *perek*, as well as additional insights and aids; *The Navi Journey* (English) by R. Ilan Ginian explains the *Navi*, *perek* by *perek*, through the insights of various commentators and luminaries. I have personally used these *sefarim* and benefited immensely from them.

ENDNOTES

[i] מורי ורבי הגאון ר' יוסף ברויער זצללה"ה ראש ישיבת פרנקפורט ונכד ר' שמשון רפאל הירש זצללה"ה היה אומר כי נביאים ראשונים יכולים ללמוד רק ילדים צעירים או תלמידי חכמים גדולים, כי הבינונים לא יוכלו להבין את כל העניינים הקשים הנמצאים שם.

[ii] מטל שחרותי נצטערתי על שדעתי קצרה להבין אף פשוטו של מקרא, וביחוד הרגשתי קושי בלמוד הנ"ך שאין מורה ומלמד ואין מסורה איך ללמוד אותה ומועטים המעיינים בו. והייתי תאב ונפשי חשקה לדעת ולהשיג אותה, והרבה שנים גרסה נפשי לתאוה, ויתברך הבורא וישתבח היוצר שאחרי שחזרתי על ספרי מגילות כמה פעמים התחלתי לטעום מנופת צופה ונפתח לי פתח להבנתה, והתחלתי לראות הצלחה בלימודי, ובמשך השנים יגעתי ומצאתי... ואף שעדיין רחוקה היא ממני מכל מקום ראיתי ברכה וסייעתא דשמיא בעמלי.

[iii] מרן הגאון הצדיק ר' אליהו לופיאן זללה"ה קבל בקבלות ל'ועדים' שלו, שיש ללמוד פעם בשבוע פרק אחד בנ"ך. הרגיל בספרי מוסר יודע כיצד רבינו יונה, רבינו בחיי, והרמח"ל למדו מפסוקים יסודות גדולות ונפלאים בעבודת השם, ובדרכם נלך גם אנחנו בלמדנו נ"ך. מה טוב ללמוד נ"ך עם תרגום יונתן בן עוזיאל, תלמידו הגדול של הלל הזקן, כי מי כמוהו גילה את ביאורי הכתובים שהיו מקובלים אצל התנאים. מלבד הפירושים על הנ"ך, יש ללמוד על כל פרשה את הילקוט שמעוני להתלמד ממנו איך חז"ל למדו את הנ"ך.

[iv] אם תלמד כל יום גם פרק בנ"ך, מה טוב ומה נעים. וכמו שכתב רש"י הקדוש בפרשת תשא (לא:יח), 'ויתן אל משה ככלתו וגו', מה כלה מתקשטת בכ"ד קישוטין... אף תלמיד חכם צריך להיות בקי בכ"ד ספרים'.

A Few Words on
"Derech HaLimud"
When Studying *Tanach*

HERE ARE MANY DIFFERENT ways to study *Tanach*, depending on one's personal interest, one's level of general Torah-knowledge, the pace at which one wants to progress through the text, etc. Hashem, in His infinite wisdom and kindness, provided us with a Torah that can be explained on a plethora of levels, studied in widely different manners, and understood by all students, young and old, simple and sophisticated. As long as we engage in our study with requisite "fear of Heaven" and with the ultimate goal of heeding God's will and following His ways,[1] we can each find a personal path in Torah

---

1. To correctly understand the Torah, one must follow the rules prescribed by the very Author of that Torah. It is clear from numerous sources (see, for example, *Tehillim* 111:10 and *Avos* 3:9) that "fear of Heaven" (*yiras Shamayim*) — a humbling deference to Divine omniscience and omnipotence — is required in order to attain a proper understanding of the Torah's ideas. (For an explanation of why this is true, see the Gra's comments on *Mishlei* 1:7.)

For practical guidelines regarding how one may or may not approach his study, see *Rambam* (*Hilchos Avodah Zarah*, ch. 2). (A competent Rabbi should be consulted for more detailed instruction.) As for the degree to which one should explicitly focus on "fear of Heaven" while studying (as opposed to more

that most directly speaks to our individual personalities and capabilities.[2]

Generally, my personal approach to studying *Tanach* focuses on trying to decipher some of the deeper messages and ideas that the Torah is conveying through the text and storyline. The crux of this style of learning is outlined nicely by a student of R. Moshe Shapira *zt"l*, R. Alexander Mandelbaum (*Mi'Maamakim*, vol. 1, pp. 8–10):[i]

It is not easy to expose what which The Ancient One (Hashem) disguised in layer upon layer of camouflage. Had our Sages not come and explicated the Torah, we would not have been able to understand the essence of Torah at all... but even the words of the Sages require much elucidation, as they too disguised their words in camouflage, in the manner of parables and riddles, in a manner that makes it difficult to appreciate the depths of their intentions.[3] "The manner of our Sages is to reveal lofty concepts in language that seems mundane... Nothing of our Sages'

---

subconsciously allowing this sense to guide one's learning), see R. Chaim Volozhiner's directive (*Nefesh HaChaim* 4:6–9).

The Rambam (*Hilchos Yesodei HaTorah* 4:13) also stresses that, for one to properly understand Torah thought and philosophy, one must first master Talmudic logic and law. Such study shapes one's mind to think in accordance with Godly wisdom. It is no accident that the most famous and influential Biblical commentators (Rashi, Ramban, and others) were also among the greatest and most influential Talmudists. [Many have pointed out that much academic "Bible scholarship" has unfortunately been plagued with deficiencies in these areas, lacking the requisite deferential attitude, solid Talmudic background, and profound understanding of Torah logic and law.]

2. The Gemara states (*Avodah Zarah* 19a): אין אדם לומד אלא מה שלבו חפץ — "A person learns only that which his heart desires." The Chafetz Chaim (*Shem Olam*, vol. 1, ch. 13) beautifully develops the idea that each individual was given a unique part of the Torah. R. Yisrael Salanter (*Ohr Yisrael*, #30, s.v. ובזה יתבאר ענין בית שמאי ובית הלל) further explains that people have varied personalities and will ultimately see the Torah from different perspectives.

3. The Maharal emphasizes this point throughout his works. See, for example, *Gur Aryeh* (*Beshalach* 15:26, Mechon Yerushalayim ed., fn. 206).

[teachings] does not make us wiser, in every manner and respect, whether in halachah or *aggadah*. In most instances, we do not scrape the surface of that to which they [our Sages] allude" ([quoted] in the name of Ramchal).

Now God shone light from the east [in the form of] our mentor and teacher R. Yehuda Loew, known as [the] Maharal [of Prague], who lit a path toward [understanding] the words of our Sages. The central point in his (the Maharal's) approach is to explain the profound meaning of the words of our Sages, as per the root [i.e., the essence] of the concepts. He (the Maharal) writes (*Sanhedrin* 82b)... "The practice of the Sages is to speak of the essence... This is well understood by every wise and knowledgeable individual: that the Sages spoke of 'essence' alone. [To illustrate,] if a man spots an individual with but four fingers — for this individual never received a physical fifth finger — a wise man would recognize that this [four-fingered] individual's essence includes a head, two ears, ten fingers, and ten toes. Is this false?! Certainly this is completely correct! On the contrary, would he (the observer) state that this [four-fingered] individual's essence includes [only] nine fingers, *that* would be false, for the missing finger relates not to his essence but rather to circumstance, that his physical being was not fitting to receive [a tenth finger]. But his fundamental essence remains that of a ten-fingered man."

R. Eliyahu Dessler *zt"l* (*Michtav Me'Eliyahu*, vol. 5, p. 401) summarizes this approach succinctly: "The essence of studying *Nach* is to learn the inner depths of its topics."[ii]

Admittedly, due to my limited knowledge and understanding, I am sure that I usually do not merit reaching even an iota of the true depth of the Torah — that which true Torah giants (such as R. Shapira and R. Dessler) can attain. Nevertheless, I try to live my life by *Chazal*'s adage (*Avos* 2:16), "לא עליך המלאכה לגמור ולא אתה בן חורין להבטל ממנה" — we are not expected to finish all the work that needs to be done (and to understand the depth of all parts of Torah), but we are nonetheless required to try our best to accomplish what we can.[4] I therefore learn the text and various *sefarim* that I can find on each topic with an acceptance that I will almost certainly not truly plumb the depths of any given topic.

In truth, all serious students of Torah sense these limitations when they engage in genuine study. The late Telzer Rosh Yeshivah, R. Yosef Yehudah Leib Bloch *zt"l* (*Shiurei Da'as*, vol. 1 [Feldheim Publishers, 5749], pp. 20–21), offers a profound understanding of this phenomenon in his instruction on how Torah should be studied:[iv]

> A person must adopt a measured approach [to the study of Torah] in order not to [on the one hand] compromise his understanding or the level of comprehension that he is able to attain, and also in order not to [on the other hand] exceed the degree [of depth of understanding] that befits him. Rather, one's progress in [grasping] the content of the Torah should advance in increments; one should progress in synchronous step with the Torah that he has [thus far] understood, and he should enter [only] those worlds in which he can deliberate. To know both [1] that one is not toiling less than he should in order to reach the understanding appropriate for his soul's capacity (i.e. that one is not underachieving), and [2] that one is not skipping ahead of his tier and leaving his sphere (i.e., that one is not overshooting) — there are two litmus tests:
>
> The first test: If one's thinking is correct and is focused on knowing the Torah, and if one's conclusions are correct, they [his final conclusions] must conform to plain reality. Even if one is unable to find solid reasoning and understanding [for a Torah law] through one's initial legal-style logic, one must delve deeper to decipher the Torah's [true] meaning, such that [the Torah's] reasoning, founded upon lofty wisdom, pierces the layers of [human] thought and [yet] simultaneously conforms to simple,

---

4. R. Eliyahu Dessler *zt"l* (*Michtav Me'Eliyahu*, vol. 5, p. 264) writes that it is utterly incorrect for one to even think that he can complete his tasks in this world. A man's obligation is to try, to toil; not to *complete*.[iii]

straightforward reasoning and common sense. For it is not considered a complete [grasp of] Torah unless [one's understanding of the Torah] resonates with one's whole essence...

The second test: The wisdom of the Torah reflects the correct outlook regarding the entirety of creation, which begins with the foundation of material being and penetrates all worlds. Moreover, the Torah itself never changes, on any planes of its meaning — from its root and origin encapsulating its deepest secrets down to its outermost layer ("clothing") in which it (the profundity of the Torah) cloaks itself by way of detailed laws and simple reasoning for its commandments. Hence, the Torah contains no idea regarding which a person will not feel that there is yet more (deeper) meaning; rather, it (one's current best understanding) opens [doors] for one to find new avenues [of meaning] to contemplate more and more, endlessly. So, when a person's comprehension of the [Torah's] reasoning rises and becomes clearer in his heart and clarified in his mind, deeper avenues ("gates") of the [wisdom of the] Torah will open instantly and more refined paths of thought will stretch before him. And even as the ideas in his mind crystallize, he will feel that the [Torah's] reasoning has yet much room to widen and broaden, as he still stands at but the beginning of comprehension. And [throughout this process and by not misrepresenting the Torah's teachings,] Hashem's Torah remains *"temimah"* (pure, complete, whole, and flawless), as he (the student of the Torah) did not detract from it at all... [Even] when one achieves the fullest capacity of his own individual understanding, it (the Torah) continues to expand beyond [those] limits.

When a person senses this, he will know that even though he must refrain from delving further into deep thought so as not to exceed the realm of his comprehension, nevertheless, that which he did not cognitively grasp and mentally achieve remains true and correct.

Hence, even when students such as myself cannot grasp the deepest of messages hidden within a text, we can nonetheless discover a degree of the inner workings of a story, albeit on a less lofty, more practical plane. And in fact, this understanding can often serve as a stepping-stone via which we can eventually, as we learn more and mature spiritually, comprehend even deeper ideas when exposed to them. A thinking person should certainly have a more developed understanding of Torah as a young adult than he did as a child, and he should have an even more developed understanding as an older, more mature and knowledgeable adult than he did in his younger years.[5] Rabbeinu Bachya ibn Paquda (*Chovos HaLevavos, Sha'ar Cheshbon HaNefesh*, ch. 3, s.v. והארבעה ועשרים) indeed instructs that one should study *Tanach* anew once one's mind has matured:[v]

> Do not be content with the [simplistic] fashion in which you pictured complex ideas and deep concepts when you first began to study. Rather, when your intellect and perception mature, you should start [over again] to examine God's Torah and the books of His prophets as one who has never studied so much as one letter from them. And condition yourself to define and explain them — to contemplate their words and phraseology, what makes sense in context, what should be taken literally and what should not be taken literally, what is straightforward and what is esoteric, what can be legitimately compared and what cannot.

R. Yosef Yehudah Leib Bloch *zt"l* (*Shiurei Da'as*, op. cit., pp. 15–16) expands upon this point:[vi]

> One of limited [spiritual or intellectual] stature, unable to elevate himself above this lowly world, can understand the Torah only on its simplest and most obvious level, inasmuch as it (the Torah) is linked to matters of the lowly world. One who rises further

---

5. R. Alexander Mandelbaum (*Mi'Maamakim*, vol. 1, p. 8) laments the fact that many people do not seek to understand *Tanach* on a level deeper than they were taught as youngsters. R. Yitzchak Isaac Sher *zt"l*, the late Rosh Yeshiva of Slabodka, develops this point as well (see introduction to his work, *Avraham Avinu*).

and reaches more lofty worlds can link those very explanations to those [loftier] worlds that he is able to access. Those very same explanations [that were accessible to him at the Torah's simplest level of understanding] broaden and expand; the principles and particulars that he sensed from afar and visualized but dimly and through an unlit prism broaden and expand before him and enlighten him with a bright, clear, and glowing light. Moreover, new previously unfathomed fountains of wisdom burst open before him...[6] Now, the path that ascends upward in holiness has no dimensions or end; there is no limit to the heights one can reach, [ascending] from one achievement to the next, as our Sages remarked (end of Tractate *Berachos*), "Torah scholars find respite neither in this world nor in the next."

Similarly, *Chazal* instruct (*Avodah Zarah* 19a) that one have multiple teachers and *rabbeim* in order to gain various perspectives and wide-ranging degrees of understanding.[7] It is recorded of great men that even as they were highly accomplished Torah scholars, they nonetheless continued searching, well into their later years, for new *rabbeim* to teach them perspectives and deeper aspects of the Torah to which they had not yet been exposed.[8]

Yet there are times when one tries hard to understand the words of *Chazal* and nevertheless cannot make sense of them. R. Eliyahu Dessler *zt"l* (*Michtav Me'Eliyahu*, vol. 4, pp. 353–4) assuages such concerns and explains that a student may continue to learn

---

6. R. Yehoshua Hartman *shlita*, based on the words of the Maharal (see Mechon Yerushalayim ed. of *Gur Aryeh, Bechukosai* 26:3, fn. 8), adds that the mitzvah of Torah study is unique in that each newly comprehended aspect of the Torah represents a novel mitzvah ("new Torah" of sorts), as opposed to a mere repetition of a previously performed mitzvah.

7. See *Maharal* (*Chiddushei Agaddos, Avodah Zarah* ibid.); *Birkas Ya'avetz* (by R. David Cohen *shlita*, vol. 3, p. 204).

8. See the outstanding biography of R. Mosheh Twersky *Hy"d*, *A Malach in Our Midst* (ch. 5, particularly pp. 105–119).

at the level that he understands and does not need to inculcate
teachings that he does not comprehend:[vii]

> Concerning passages of *"aggadah"* that we do not understand —
> we are not obligated to study them or rely upon them in our
> service [of Hashem], even though these teachings certainly con-
> tain fundamentals of Torah [philosophy]. Not so with practical
> halachah — we are obliged to perform the commandments even
> if we cannot understand them (i.e., their rationale or purpose).
> *Aggadah,* however, aims to arouse our emotions ("enlighten our
> hearts"). Thus, inasmuch as some *aggadah* fails to do so — on
> account of our own measly capacity to comprehend — we are
> exempt from involving ourselves with it (i.e., engaging in its study
> and adopting its prescriptions) until we merit achieving the ca-
> pacity to understand it... For we cannot utilize *aggadic* teachings
> to guide our service of Hashem if we do not understand them
> (i.e., what they are trying to teach us)... After all, how can we rely
> on something whose meaning still eludes us, especially when it is
> quite probable that the true meaning of the passage is completely
> different [than our current interpretation]? This is what Rashi,
> Radak, and others mean when they write that a particular *derash*
> (*midrashic* interpretation) lies at odds with the *peshat* (more lit-
> eral meaning of a passage) or is inadequate; namely, we cannot
> apply such a *midrashic* interpretation until we clarify and com-
> prehend [the wisdom of] its substance.

Regarding methodology for understanding the text itself, there
are many different avenues that one could take to understand
Tanach. Some commentators dedicate their works to the literal
meaning of the text (*peshat*), while others focus on hidden meaning
that lies well beneath the surface (*derash, sod,* etc.).[9] Some people

---

9. R. Moshe Yechiel Epstein *zt"l* (*Aish Dos,* vol. 5, 3:1:10, p. 170) notes that these
multiple facets of Torah exposition (referred to as *"Pardes"*) exist in *all* books of
Tanach, not only in the Five Books of the Torah.

base their understandings primarily on the interpretation of *Chazal* (found in Gemara, Midrash, etc.); others often deviate from *Chazal's* explanation of the text, noting that the Torah allows for alternative commentary in realms such as *Tanach* and *Aggadah*, as long as such commentary does not carry with it practical ramifications that run contrary to the accepted law (halachah).[10]

These various modes of understanding need not stand at odds with one another. They can, and ideally *should*, complement each other. Each interpretation reveals a unique aspect of the wisdom of the Torah and illustrates the Torah's vastness and all-encompassing nature. R. Yehudah Cooperman (*Peshuto shel Mikra*, vol. 2, p. 80) stresses this point:[viii]

> There is no difference — with respect to the holiness of the Torah — between the *peshat*, *midrash*, *remez*, and *sod*. Each of these [modes

---

10. For example, see *Ohr HaChaim* (introduction, s.v. ולפעמים); R. Shmuel Ha-Nagid's *Mevo HaTalmud* (s.v. והגדה) with explanation of *Michtav Me'Eliyahu* (vol. 4, pp. 354–5); *Ramban* (opening comments to *Bereishis* 8:4). See also the Torah journal *Ohr Yisrael* (vol. 13, pp. 214–5) where the author argues that this sentiment is evident from most, if not all, classic commentators of *Tanach*. For further discussion of the halachic basis for such exegesis, see *Beis Yishai* (*Derashos*, ch. 15, pp. 126–8).

Sifsei Chaim (*Emunah U'Bechirah*, vol. 2, pp. 259–272) explains that the *peshat*, even when explained contrary to the halachah or to the historical tradition recorded by our Sages, contains important aspects of truth and enhances one's understanding of the concepts that the Torah wishes to convey. R. Yehudah Cooperman (*Peshuto shel Mikra*, vol. 1, sec. 1; commentary on *Meshech Chochmah*, *Pirkei Mevo*) echoes this idea as he highlights the many teachings that are gleaned from a proper understanding of *peshat*.

It should be stressed, however, that this approach has its limits. Explaining the Torah in a fashion that contradicts various tenets is often forbidden, foolish, and false. Understanding the parameters of expounding the Torah's text usually requires guidance from *rabbeim*, a somewhat broad sense of Rabbinic commentary and tradition, and sincere fear of Heaven. For more on this issue, see R. Netanel Wiederblank *shlita*'s essay, "The Limits of Interpretation: Are There Red Lines in *Peshat*?" (*Jewish Action*, Winter 2018).

of interpretation] reveals to us various aspects of holiness and wholeness of the Torah.[11]

Indeed, the Gra (*Mishlei* 2:9)[ix] comments that one does not fully comprehend *peshat* unless he also understands the deeper meaning of the text.[12] The Gra adds (as quoted by R. Uriel Schonberg, *Ohr Tzafun: Bei'ur HaHoshanos*, ch. 20)[x] that one's exposition of the *peshat* of the Torah should include allusions to the deeper "secrets" hidden within the *peshat*.

Furthermore, R. Schonberg (ibid.) explains that even the realm of *peshat* contains multiple levels of explication of the Torah's text — "*pardes* of *peshat*."[13] In fact, the very definition of *peshat* is a matter of serious debate (see R. Kasher's *Torah Sheleimah*,

---

11. R. Cooperman laments the fact that many academics see only *peshat* as "*the correct interpretation*" and that others view *midrash* as "*the true peshat*." In truth, however, both *midrash* and *peshat* are imperative for fully grasping the infinite wisdom of the Torah.

12. See also *Afikei Mayim* (*Sefiras HaOmer U'Shavuos*, pp. 41–2), *Sifsei Chaim* (ibid. p. 268), and *Peshuto shel Mikra* (R. Cooperman, vol. 1, pp. 196–9) for further elaboration. In a similar vein, the Maharal, in numerous places, stresses that a *derashah* (Rabbinic interpretation of *Tanach* founded upon textual clues), when understood properly, is not a *deviation* from *peshat*, but in fact represents a *deeper understanding* of *peshat*, as the *derashah* illuminates hidden levels of the text itself. He therefore stresses that a profound understanding of a *derashah* must be rooted in the very text of *Tanach*. For elucidation of this idea and for numerous examples of this phenomenon noted by the Maharal, see R. Yehoshua Hartman's edition of *Gur Aryeh* (vol. 9, introduction, pp. 15–19, 24–27).

R. Shimon Schwab *zt"l* (*Ma'ayan Beis HaSho'evah, Bereishis* 1:1) further notes that there seem to be verses of the Torah that cannot be explained satisfactorily without assuming that the Torah is hinting at a deeper layer of exposition. Similarly, some point to various sections of *Tanach* that are intended to be read, even initially, on the level of *derash*, etc. See the comments of R. Moshe Eisemann (Artscroll *Tanach* Series, *Yechezkel* 44:17) and the *Maharatz Chayes* (*Kol Sifrei Maharatz Chayes*, vol. 1, *Mevo HaTalmud*, ch. 22).

13. For additional sources addressing this concept, see *Paradise* (by R. Elchanan Shoff, introduction, fn. 3).

vol. 17, appendix #22). According to many commentators, even *peshat* can sometimes contain aspects of *aggadic* and non-literal interpretation. That is, there can be many valid readings of any particular text, with some of those readings being more apparent than others. But all layers of interpretation, transparent and subtle alike, work together to create a marvelous tapestry of wisdom. One can, while explaining the Torah on a "simple level," simultaneously strive to delve deeper and open avenues to further levels of understanding, even without fully developing (or even comprehending) those more sublime ideas.

Consistent with my aforementioned general objective when learning *Tanach*, I try to grasp the words of the *Navi* on the deepest plane that is within my scope of comprehension. And I try to do so in a fashion that emanates from the words of the *Navi* itself. It is therefore necessary to consider both the simple meaning of the text (based on the wording of the *Navi* along with some of the various commentaries) *and* ideas that do not necessarily stem from the text.

In a sense, I try to balance *peshat* with ideas that would not necessarily be initially defined as such. Excessive focus on the technical details of the text can sometimes blind the reader to more fundamental messages. Moreover, one finds that even interpretations that ostensibly address only the literal *peshat* are often compelled to fill large gaps in the storyline by interposing narratives that are not apparent from the text. To this end, they evoke thoughts or describe events that are often highly debatable.[14] On the other hand, concentrating exclusively on broader ideas can lead to an understanding that has little relevance to the words of the Torah itself. Likewise, isolated analysis of comments by *Chazal*

---

14. See also *Journey Through Nach* (vol. 1, pp. 20–21) for additional drawbacks of focusing solely on literal *peshat*.

or classic commentators without any regard for the scriptural text is often misleading and incomplete. The words of *Tanach* were certainly recorded in a particular manner for a reason, and those words therefore carry great import. It seems self-evident that *Chazal* themselves did not intend for *Tanach* to be understood wholly based on their writings.[15] Rather, they intended for us to utilize the actual text of *Tanach* in conjunction with their guiding comments and tradition in order to attain a fuller picture of that which the Torah wishes to convey.[16]

---

15. It should be noted, however, that during the *Haskalah* movement, many Torah leaders advocated focusing almost solely on Rabbinic interpretation and emphatically scorned methodology that was based on nuanced reading of the text. They feared that scrutinizing the text of *Tanach* could easily lead a student to empathize with the followers of *Haskalah*. See Prof. Mordechai Breuer's article, *HaMikra BaTochnit HaLimudim shel HaYeshivah* (published in *Mechkarim BaMikra U'VaChinuch*, pp. 234–5), for quotes on this issue from Torah leaders of that era. Yet, as mentioned in the previous essay (see pp. 28–29, with footnote 10), numerous contemporary leaders and educators have determined that many past concerns are not as relevant in today's age, and they advocate and encourage earnest study of *Tanach*.

16. The Malbim (introduction to *Nach*) notes that although many of the classic Biblical commentaries focus mainly on *peshat*, it is the task of the later commentaries to build upon their works and reveal deeper meanings and nuances in the text. The early commentaries, explains the Malbim, serve as the initial, foundational works on *Tanach*, and they enable and facilitate all subsequent analysis. (See *Peninei HaParashah*, year 14, vol. 681, *Parashas Behar-Bechukosai*, for further sources supporting this idea.)

R. Cooperman (*Peshuto shel Mikra*, vol. 2, p. 82) adds that many of the *Rishonim* (Rashi, Rashbam, etc.) felt that *aggadic* material (Midrash, etc.) was readily available to the student who wished to uncover "deeper" levels of *Tanach* (as Rashi notes in his commentary on *Bereishis* 3:8, "יש מדרשי אגדה רבים, וכבר סידרום רבותינו על מכונם בבראשית רבה ובשאר המדרשות"). They therefore dedicated their works to *peshat*, with the goal of offering an essential type of commentary that did not yet exist. They saw their works as enhancing the classic works of *Chazal* by providing the basics upon which all deeper comprehension rests.

R. Chaim Friedlander *zt"l* (*Sifsei Chaim, Emunah U'Bechirah*, vol. 2, pp. 395–7) adds that earlier generations, as opposed to more recent ones, did not require

In addition to the challenges of balancing *peshat* versus *derash* and text versus conceptual analysis, students of *Tanach* are presented with another related concern — how is one meant to understand the errors of our great leaders? A completely literal understanding of many of their recorded mistakes often runs contrary to our tradition and paints inaccurately critical portraits of our revered ancestors. Such simplistic interpretations risk distorting both historical facts and the lessons that the Torah means to teach. Yet the wording of the Biblical text must also not be ignored. The *Navi* records each occurrence in a particular manner; his choice of language should not be overlooked. As described above, it is crucial to formulate an understanding based on the words of *Chazal* and the classic commentaries while concomitantly understanding why the text of the Torah was written as it was.[17]

It is critical to stress one final point. As mentioned, all Torah study must be driven by a deep sense of "fear of Heaven" and a desire to fulfill the will of the Almighty and become closer to Him. Although a student, during the actual time of study, should focus mainly on understanding the material (as described by R. Chaim Volozhiner's *Nefesh HaChaim* 4:3), his ultimate purpose

---

elaborate commentary in order to connect with the sentiments and wondrous ideas that the Torah wishes to convey.

17. I hope, with Hashem's help, to present a more detailed essay on this matter in a future publication on *Sefer Shoftim*. For the time being, let it suffice to say that when we speak of mistakes or "failures" of previous greats, we are using imprecise, "borrowed," terminology. We cannot truly comprehend the legendary figures of *Tanach*, their connection to the Almighty, or the profundity of their thought processes. Rather, we try our best to process and frame their deeds and motives in terms that we can utilize, all the while appreciating that our notions of those very deeds and motives fall significantly short of capturing their full depth and complexity. (For further explication of this approach and how it applies to numerous episodes throughout *Tanach*, see *Koros HaDoros*, by R. Tzvi Aryeh Zilber — particularly vol. 1, p. 30.)

for engaging in Torah study must be to serve and connect with his Creator (see *Nefesh HaChaim* 4:4 and onward). This axiom is especially crucial when learning *Nach*, as described nicely by R. Daniel Fine and Chaim Golker in *Journey Through Nach* (p. 22):

> The Gemara in *Megillah* (14a) tells us that there are fifty-five recorded Jewish prophets in our history — forty-eight men and seven women. Yet, notes the Gemara, there were over a million prophets across our history whose prophecies were not recorded... The Gemara reveals that only those prophecies which had relevance for future generations were recorded. One can see from here that our approach to learning these recorded prophecies is not to regard the messages as archaic, out of date, limited to "those times" and irrelevant. On the contrary, we must realize that the reason for these prophecies having been written down is that they are relevant to *us*... Indeed, the Rambam (*Hilchos Teshuvah* 4:2) writes that the purpose of the Prophets was to bring us to repentance and closeness to God... and this is why, in the times of Mashiach, all the prophecies will no longer need to be studied (see *Rambam, Hilchos Megillah* 2:18), for we will be on such a spiritual level whereby we do not need this push to repent.

May it be Hashem's will that our study of *Nach* indeed brings us closer to following His ways and to the ultimate Redemption.

ENDNOTES

[i] לא קלה היא הדרך לגלות את מה שכיסה עתיק יומין במסווה שעל גבי מסווה. אילולי באו חז"ל ופירשו את התורה, לא היינו יכולים לעמוד על עיקרה של תורה כלל... אך גם דברי חז"ל צריכים ביאור רב, שהרי גם הם כיסו את דבריהם במסווה, בדרך משל ומליצה, באופן שקשה לרדת לעומק כוונתם. 'דרכם של חז"ל היא לגלות דברים רמים וגבוהים במלים הנראים כדברים בעלמא... אין דבר בחז"ל שלא עושה אותנו יותר חכמים, בכל ענין ובכל דבר, בין בהלכה ובין באגדה. ברוב המקרים אין אנו פוגעים ואין אנו נוגעים במה שרומזים' (בשם רמח"ל).

והנה האיר ה' ממזרח, מורנו הרב רבי יהודה ליוואי, המכונה בשם מהר"ל, אשר האיר דרך בדברי חז"ל. הנקודה המרכזית בשיטתו היא לבאר את עומק הפשט בדברי חז"ל כפי

שורשי הדברים. וזה לשונו (בביאורו לאגדות הש"ס סנהדרין פ"ב ע"ב)... דרך חכמים לדבר מן המהות... והדברים מובנים מאוד לכל איש חכם ויודע כי דברי חכמים במהות בלבד, הלא כאשר יראה האדם אחד שהוא בעל ד' אצבעות שלא קבל החומר אצבע החמישית. ויאמר עליו החכם, האדם הזה מהותו שהוא בעל ראש ושני אזנים ועשר אצבעות ידים ורגלים. וכי שקר הוא. זה בודאי אמת גמור הוא. ואדרבה אם הוא אמר כי מהות זה האדם ההוא בעל ט' אצבעות הלא שקר הוא דובר, כי אצבע החסר אין זה מצד מהותו רק מצד מקרה שלא היה החומר מוכן לקבל, ומצד מהותו בעצמו הוא בעל עשר אצבעות.

[ii] העיקר בלימוד נ"ך: ללמוד פנימיות הענינים.

[iii] אם חושב אדם לעשות - מוטב. אבל החושב לגמור מלאכתו - זה אפיקורסות. לא עליך המלאכה לגמור, כי אי אפשר לאדם לגמור כלל. אדם נולד באמצע ענין ומסתלק באמצע ענין, ואין 'גמירה' בגדר אדם כלל. ועל כן אין לו לחשוב חשבונות בעבודתו בעולמו כמה יבנה ויגמור ויתקן. המציב לו תכלית כזו - טועה. כי התכלית - עבודת ה', עמל... וכל מעשה ומעשה בעבודת ה' הוא הוא התכלית.

[iv] האדם צריך ללמוד את מדתו ולפלס את מעגל דרכו כדי שלא יפחית את מדת הבנתו וערך קומתו בהבנת התורה, וגם שלא יפריז על המדה הראויה לו. אלא שהתעלותו בדברי התורה תלך בהדרגה, שיתעלה הוא ביחד עם דברי התורה שהגיע עדיהם, ויכנס בעולמות ההם שהוא דן בהם. וכדי לדעת את שתי הידיעות אם אינו פוחת במדת עמלו הדרוש לו כדי שיגיע למחשבתו הנכונה כפי מתכונת נשמתו, ואם אינו קופץ למעלה ממדרגתו ויוצא מעגולו, יש לזה ב' בחינות.

בחינה הראשונה: אם מחשבתו נכונה ומכוונת לדעת התורה ומסקנותיו אמתיות הנה, צריכות הן להתאים עם המציאות הפשוטה. ואף שאם יתחיל לחקור רק בהגיון משפטי לא ימצא את הטעם ולא יבינהו, מכל מקום אחרי שהתעמק לכוון דעת התורה, צריך הטעם, המיוסד על יסודי החכמה העליונה, לחדור דרך שכבות המחשבה, ולהתאים גם כן עם ההבנה הפשוטה וישר ההגיון האתחלתי. כי אין זו תורה שלמה אם לא ירגישנה האדם וימצא בה טעם בכל מהותו...

בחינה השניה: מכיון שדעת התורה היא הכונה הנכונה בכל מציאות הבריאה, המתחלת משורש המציאות וחוזרת דרך כל העולמות, ולא עוד אלא שהתורה עצמה אינה משתנית בכל אפני הבנתה, משרשה ותחלתה על פי רזי דרזין שלה עד הלבוש, שבו היא מתלבשת בפרטי דיניה וטעמי מצוותיה הפשוטים, אם כן אין לך סברת התורה שלא ירגיש בה האדם כי הטעם אינו נגמר ונפסק, אלא פותח הוא לו למוצאו דרך לחשוב יותר ויותר עד בלי סוף. וכשיתעלה יותר בהבנת הטעם ויתברר לו, יכון בלבו ויתבהר בשכלו, מיד יפתחו לו שערי תורה יותר עמוקים ויתפשטו אפקי מחשבה יותר עדינים. ואף כשמושגי שכלו יאספו, ירגיש כי הסברא עדיין מתרחבת ומתפשטת והוא עומד בתחלת ההשגה, ותורת ה' עדיין תמימה ולא החסיר ממנה כלום... כשיגיע האדם עד סוף מחשבתו והיא עדיין נמשכת למעלה משעור קומתו.

וכשירגישם האדם את זאת ידע כי אף שהוא צריך להפסיק מלכת יותר בעומק המחשבה, למען לא יצא מן מעגולו, מכל מקום מה שתפס במחשבתו והגיע בעומק הבנתו הוא אמת ונכון.

[v] אל תנוח דעתך על מה שנצטייר בלבך בתחלת לימודך מן הענינים המסופקים והסברות העמוקות. אבל ראוי לך להתחיל בעת חזוק שכלך והכרתך לעיין בספר תורת האלקים וספרי

נביאיו כמי שלא למד מהם אות. ותרגיל עצמך לפרשם ולבארם ולהתבונן במלותם ובלשונם, ומה שסובלות מן הענינים, ומה שיש מהם כפשוטו ומה שאינו כפשוטו, ומה שיש מהם נראה ומה שהוא מהם נסתר, ומה שההקשה נמצאת בו ומה שאין ההקשה נמצאת בו.

[vi] מי ששיעור קומתו קטן ואינו עולה למעלה מעולמו זה התחתון, יכול להבין את התורה רק על פי פשוטה וגלויה, כפי שהיא מקושרת עם עניני העולם התחתון. ומי שמתעלה יותר ומגיע לעולמות יותר גבוהים, הוא מוצא בו בעצמו אותן הסברות לפי התקשרותן לעולמות ההם שהגיע עדיהם, אותן הסברות עצמן מתרחבות ומתפשטות, הכללים והחלוקים שהרגיש אותם מרחוק והאירו לפניו באור כהה ובאספקלריא שאינה מאירה, מתרחבים לפניו ומתפשטים ומאירים לעיניו באור גדול, בהיר ומזהיר. ולא עוד אלא שמעיינות של חכמה חדשים נבקעים לפניו אשר לא שערם מראשו... והנה הדרך העולה למעלה בקדש אין לה שיעור וערך כלל ואין קץ למעלות האדם שיוכל ללכת אל חיל, וכמה שאמרו חז"ל (סוף גמ' ברכות) 'תלמידי חכמים אין להם מנוחה לא בעולם הזה ולא בעולם הבא'.

[vii] פירשנו דבריו (של ר' שמואל הנגיד במבוא התלמוד) דבדברי אגדה אשר לא נבינם אין אנו מחוייבים ללמוד אותם ולסמוך עבודתנו עליהם, אם כי ברור שהם יסודות התורה. אבל ההלכה שהיא למעשה הרי מחוייבים הרי במעשה המצוות אנו גם לא נבינם. אבל האגדה שהיא באה להאיר לבב, הרי כל זמן שאינה מארת לנו (מפני קטנות השגתנו) אין אנו מחוייבים להתעסק בה, עד שנזכה ונעלה למדרגה שנבין אותה... מפני שאי אפשר לנו לעבוד את ה' בלבבנו על פיהם אם לא נבינם. ואם כן איך נסמוך על דבר שלא נדע עדיין פירושו ומסתמא כוונת המאמר אחרת היא לגמרי. ועל דרך זה הוא אשר כתבו רש"י ורד"ק ועוד שזה הדרש רחוק מהפשט או אינו מיושב, דהיינו שלא נוכל להשתמש בו טרם נבין אותו ויתבררו לנו דבריו.

[viii] אין הבדל בקדושת התורה בין הפשט, המדרש, הרמז, והסוד. אלה ואלה מגלים לנו את הפנים השונות של הקדושה והשלמות של תורה.

[ix] כל זמן שלא יבין הסוד, אפילו הפשט אינו ברור בידו, כמ"ש בזוהר משפטים.

[x] הוסיף הגר"א (שיר השירים ד:יא) שהדרך הנכונה להצניע את חכמת האמת נרמזת בפסוק 'דבש וחלב תחת לשונך'. ושמעתי שכוונת הגר"א היא ללמדנו שהאופן של ההצנעה הוא, שכאשר מדברים בפשטי התורה, הפשט יהא מכוון לסוד, ובזה נמצא הסוד מוצנע בתוך הפשט. וזה ה'דבש וחלב' (סודות התורה) 'תחת לשונך' (תחת כל דיבור של פשט)... יש כמה וכמה מדרגות ללבושים שמצמיעים את הסוד. וכידוע שיש מ"ט פנים לתורה, וגם ע' פנים לתורה, וכן הלבושים של פרד"ס הם בעצמם מורכבים מהרבה מדרגות, כגון למדרגת הפשט יש 'פרד"ס', דהיינו פשט שבפשט, ורמז שבפשט, ודרוש שבפשט וכו', עד שנמצא שכל 'פרד"ס' נעשה לבוש ל'פרד"ס' שמעליו.

SEFER
YEHOSHUA

PERAKIM 1–4:

Life after Moshe; Yehoshua's Challenge

T HE BACKDROP OF *SEFER YEHOSHUA*, the opening book of *Nach*, marks a stark historical and spiritual departure from the stage set in the preceding Five Books of the Torah. *Sefer Yehoshua* describes Bnei Yisrael's efforts to relate the Torah's wisdom to "real life" in a way that they were not previously challenged to do. While living in the desert directly under Hashem's wing — eating *mann* (manna) that Hashem provided daily, protected by His supernatural fire and cloud, etc. — Bnei Yisrael were not forced to apply the Torah to regular, mundane life. Furthermore, during Moshe Rabbeinu's lifetime, Bnei Yisrael enjoyed a constant pipeline to Hashem, as Moshe's level of prophecy was the highest that any human can possibly attain. With a leader who represented Torah itself (the Torah is even sometimes referred to as "the Torah of Moshe"![1]), Bnei Yisrael were not fully confronted with the task of applying the lofty concepts that they had been taught. Only once Moshe passed and Hashem's manifest

---

1. See, for example, *Yehoshua* 8:31–32 and 23:6; *Melachim II* 14:6.

protection and sustenance ceased were Bnei Yisrael challenged to fully embrace the Torah and relate it to daily routines, practices, and dilemmas.

Torah after Moshe

HENCE, *SEFER YEHOSHUA* represents the next stage in our nation's comprehension and observance of Torah. Yehoshua was charged with leading Bnei Yisrael in this task of converting the Torah from theory to practice.[2] In a sense, *Sefer Yehoshua* "completes"

---

2. R. Moshe Shapira *zt"l* (*Afikei Mayim: Beis HaMikdash, Churban, U'Nechamah*, pp. 147; 249–51) explores a similar idea (with the remarkable depth and style for which he is well known) regarding the evolution of Torah through other stages in history. He describes that, as the Jewish People drift chronologically farther and farther from the lofty experience at Har Sinai, the Torah needs to be "translated" to words and concepts that can be understood on progressively "lower" spiritual planes. Over the course of history, Divine wisdom is presented to mankind in various manners and through varying degrees of human input in order to relate the Torah to people living in a constantly evolving world. He explains that this idea accounts for the uniqueness of *Sefer Devarim* in relation to the rest of the Torah, for the distinctiveness of the period in which prophecy was prevalent in contradistinction to the era that followed, for the differences between the times when halachic disagreement was rare and the period during which it was prevalent, and so forth with respect to many historical ages. (See also *Afikei Mayim: Chanukah U'Purim*, ch. 1; *Pri Tzaddik: Bereishis, Ma'amar Kedushas Shabbos #7*, pp. 19b–20a s.v. ואסתר.)

R. Chaim Volozhiner (*Ruach Chaim*, R. Goldberg ed., p. 15) explains the wording of the Mishnah (*Avos* 1:1) with a similar idea. Whereas the Mishnah states that Moshe *bequeathed* (מסר) the Torah to Yehoshua, it implies that the Torah was subsequently more seamlessly transferred from Yehoshua to the elders and from the elders to the later prophets. Only the later prophets needed to "bequeath" the Torah yet again to the next generation — the *Anshei Kenesses HaGedolah*. Moshe was on his own unique plane; although he "bequeathed" the entire Torah to Yehoshua, Yehoshua was unable to wholly "receive" it (i.e., to grasp its full depth; see *Ruach Chaim*, ibid., fn. 8). Yehoshua therefore "translated" the Heavenly Wisdom to terms that he could understand. Yehoshua, the elders, and the later prophets, however, were all situated on similar planes of comprehension. They therefore transferred the Torah, as it provides an added and indispensable dimension to our perception of and adherence to the Torah.[3]

With this understanding, it is apparent why the famous directive to focus intently and constantly on the Torah's commands and on Torah study (1:8, "והגית בו יומם ולילה") was first uttered to Yehoshua and was not included in the Torah itself. It was Yehoshua who bore the unique responsibility of applying the Torah to the myriad dimensions of mundane life through constant Torah study.[4] *Chazal* write (*Yerushalmi, Horayos* 3:5; see *Mishbetzos Zahav*, p. 313) that Yehoshua, unlike Moshe, had to "toil" in the study of Torah. With Moshe gone, the nation could no longer rely upon Moshe's direct access to Hashem; the Jews would need to work and to sweat in order to understand the Torah.[5] Likewise, the

---

the Torah smoothly from one generation to the next without further "translation." But the transition from the era of prophecy to the era that followed constituted yet another drastic shift. The post-prophetic generations, too, were "bequeathed" the Torah but did not fully comprehend it to the degree that was conveyed to them by their spiritually superior predecessors.

3. The idea that *Sefer Yehoshua* "completes" the Torah can be gleaned from Rashi's opening comments to the *Sefer*. Rashi notes that the *Navi* added the letter *vav* (meaning "and") to the first word of the *Sefer* in order to link *Sefer Yehoshua* with the Five Books of the Torah. (For further clarification, see *Rinas Yitzchak* 1:1.) This idea may also be discerned from *Chazal's* statement (*Nedarim* 22b; see also Maharal's comments ad loc.) that, in a more ideal world, the only books of *Tanach* that would exist would be the Five Books of the Torah and *Sefer Yehoshua*, which forms an "addendum" of sorts to the Torah. (It should be noted, however, that all wisdom is certainly contained in the Five Books of the Torah alone. The "addendum" presented in the form of *Sefer Yehoshua* merely provides humans further opportunity to understand the ideas that are already extant, albeit sometimes hidden, in the Torah itself.)

4. Commentators similarly write that, whereas Moshe paralleled the fully set, immutable "Written Torah," Yehoshua personified the "Oral Torah," given to man to comprehend, utilize, and develop further (see *Pri Tzaddik: Bereishis, Ma'amar Kedushas Shabbos* #7, p. 20a, s.v. ובמתן).

5. As mentioned above, different stages in history demand varying degrees of mental and spiritual effort to grasp the word of Hashem. Although prophecy

famous dictum "לא בשמים היא" that instructs man to use his own capabilities to decipher the Torah and not to rely on prophecy was also seemingly applied for the first time by Yehoshua (as recorded in *Temurah* 16a).

Daunting Mission

ASIDE FROM REVOLUTIONIZING the nation's approach to the Torah and its study, Yehoshua was asked to assume Moshe's leadership duties. In a sense, Yehoshua was expected to perform the impossible: to fill the unfillable shoes of Moshe Rabbeinu. Moshe was literally one of a kind: he was the greatest prophet who ever lived and who ever will live, and he forged a connection between the Jewish nation and Hashem that no one else could have created.[6] The commentators add (see citations in *Mishbetzos Zahav*, pp. 3; 330) that, had Moshe been the one to lead Bnei Yisrael into Eretz Yisrael and conquer the land, the endeavor would have been suffused with such immense holiness that the Beis HaMikdash would never have been destroyed. Moreover, people would never have forgotten (nor would they *ever* forget) Torah that they had learned

---

remained widespread in Yehoshua's time and people were still able to ask Hashem for assistance in understanding His will, the gap between Moshe's prophecy and Yehoshua's prophecy was vast. Accordingly, a need arose in Yehoshua's age for human initiative that was unnecessary beforehand.

6. The Rambam famously includes as one of his Thirteen Principles of Jewish faith the dictum that Moshe was the greatest prophet who ever lived and who ever will live. The Maharal (*Gur Aryeh*, final comments on *Rashi, Shemos* 18:1 s.v.למשה ולישראל) adds that Moshe's wisdom encompassed and incorporated the manifold outlooks of each and every Jew. This characteristic enabled Moshe to partner with each member of the nation and assist each individual in cultivating a unique relationship with his Creator (see *Rashi* on *Bamidbar* 27:16 and fn. 87 in Machon Yerushalayim ed. of *Maharal* ibid.).

(or would ever learn). In fact, *Rashi* (1:2) states categorically that Yehoshua would simply not have been chosen as the leader had Moshe still been alive.

The text of the *Navi* bears witness to the extent of Yehoshua's challenges. Hashem instructed Yehoshua numerous times (1:6, 7, 9), *"chazak ve'ematz"* — you will need to be exceedingly strong to accomplish the impossible! This exhortation came not only from Hashem, but from Bnei Yisrael as well. They, too, appreciated the enormity of Yehoshua's mission (as implied from Gemara *Temurah* discussed below), and they, too, prodded Yehoshua, *"chazak ve'ematz"* (1:18). Bnei Yisrael even invoked a thinly veiled threat, claiming that they would follow Yehoshua's lead only if his leadership proved reminiscent of Moshe's (see 1:17 and *Metzudos David* ad loc.)!

Comprehending the Challenge

FOR YEHOSHUA TO succeed in his colossal task, and, indeed, for him to appreciate the vastness of his assignment, he needed first to recognize the magnitude of the loss that resulted from Moshe's death. The Gemara (*Temurah* 16a; see *Rashi* and *Maharsha* ad loc.) records this issue as Yehoshua's first miscalculation. The Gemara states that, just before his passing, Moshe asked Yehoshua if he (Yehoshua) had any questions to ask him (Moshe) before he left this world. Yehoshua responded that he did not, feeling that he had never left Moshe's side and that he had already absorbed from Moshe as much wisdom as possible. The Gemara relates that Yehoshua misjudged the situation; there was certainly much yet to be gained from a conversation with Moshe! Yehoshua's response highlighted his underappreciation of the grave loss that was about to ensue. The Gemara adds that, as a consequence of Yehoshua's error, the nation started to forget parts of the Torah, a fitting punishment for undervaluing Moshe's significance and teachings.

Furious with the negative impact of Yehoshua's approach, Bnei Yisrael actually threatened to kill Yehoshua! They understood that as long as Yehoshua did not recognize the singularity of Moshe, Yehoshua could not hope to emulate Moshe and carry on his legacy.

Yehoshua learned his lesson quickly.[7] He immediately sought to bridge the gap between Moshe's leadership and his own, assuring his nation that he was in fact a worthy link to Moshe's era.[8] As explained by the *Radak* and *Ralbag* (2:1), Yehoshua's motive in dispatching spies to Yericho was precisely to boost Bnei Yisrael's confidence before their impending battle. He sought to convince his people that Hashem would continue to support them, just as He did during Moshe's time.[9] In turn, Hashem assisted Yehoshua in earning Bnei Yisrael's respect: "…so that Bnei Yisrael will know that, just as He was with Moshe, so too will He be with Yehoshua" (see 3:7).[10] And to be sure, after witnessing the miracle that Hashem

---

7. *Chazal* (*Devarim Rabbah*, end of 11:10) describe the intense sorrow Yehoshua felt when he requested to see or communicate with Moshe and realized that his Rebbe, and the profound faith that he personified, were no longer accessible.

8. Hashem Himself attested to Yehoshua's competence and capability (see *Bamidbar* 27:20).

9. In fact, the spies' final report stated simply that Hashem would allow Bnei Yisrael to win the war and that the enemy was terrified; their report lacked any descriptive or strategic detail.

[For other explanations as to why Yehoshua's dispatch of spies was legitimate and distinct from the famous sin of the spies sent a generation earlier by Moshe, see *Malbim* (2:1) and *Mishbetzos Zahav* (p. 38). For yet another reason why Yehoshua sent spies and for a deeper understanding of why Divine Providence led the spies specifically to Rachav's inn, see *Mishbetzos Zahav* (pp. 42–43), who explains that the spies' ability to distance themselves from sin under such circumstances (as mentioned by *Rashi* 6:23) provided merit and guidance for the nation's holy conquest. R. Chaim Ben-Senior (*Imrei Chein*, pp. 43–45), based on the *Chida*, explains further that the spies' mission was to investigate the spiritual impurities of the land and evaluate how Bnei Yisrael could properly infuse the land with sanctity.]

10. This point is noted by R. David Sharaby *shlita* (*Sha'arei David* on *Tanach*, concluding comments on *Sefer Yehoshua* 1:5), who explains that Hashem granted

performed for Yehoshua at the Yarden — a miracle comparable to the world-famous miracle that Hashem performed for Moshe at *Yam Suf* (4:23 explicitly equates the two) — Bnei Yisrael recognized the greatness of their new leader and "feared him just as they feared Moshe" (4:14).

Reflection of Moshe

YEHOSHUA DID SUCH a good job of filling the void left by Moshe's passing that *Chazal* characterize Yehoshua as reflecting Moshe's luminescence. (Gemara *Bava Basra* 75a likens Moshe to the sun and Yehoshua to the moon; see also Rashi's comments on *Bamidbar* 27:20.)[11] As expressed in *Journey Through Nach* (p. 25): "Yehoshua's defining feature was that he reflected Moshe's leadership and continued Moshe's legacy. In this light, we see that Yehoshua is described in the Torah as 'the helper of Moshe' (משרת משה — see *Shemos* 24:13; *Bamidbar* 11:28), paralleling the opening *pasuk* of *Sefer Yehoshua*." Correspondingly, R. Shimon Krasner *shlita* (*Nachalas Shimon*, pp. 35–36) lists a number of parallels between Yehoshua and Moshe: each of them achieved all fifty levels of "*binah*" (deep understanding);[12] each died through "Hashem's kiss";

Yehoshua a blessing that the nation should accept his sovereignty even though he was not as great as his predecessor.

11. Although the Gemara, in comparing Yehoshua to the moon, intends to highlight Yehoshua's deficiencies in relation to Moshe, we nevertheless also get a glimpse of Yehoshua's greatness from that very comparison.

12. R. Krasner cites commentators who explain that Yehoshua's very name (Yehoshua bin "Nun") hints to this achievement (the numerical value of the letter *nun* equals fifty). The Ramban (*Shemos* 33:11) similarly comments that Yehoshua's name alludes to his lofty level of understanding (*binah*, from "*bin-Nun*").

(It should be noted, however, that some maintain that no mortal, while still in this world, was offered all fifty levels of understanding; see *Rosh Hashanah* 21b and R. Osher Levene's *Jewish Wisdom in the Numbers*, pp. 297–8.)

each was "equivalent" to the entirety of Bnei Yisrael;[13] etc. Yehoshua was also the only person other than Moshe who may have penned a portion of the Five Books of the Torah (see *Bava Basra* 15a and *Makkos* 11a, where some opine that Yehoshua wrote the final eight *pesukim* of the Torah). Commentators similarly note that Hashem sometimes addressed Yehoshua in a fashion reminiscent of His address to Moshe (20:1 — "וידבר ה' אל יהושע לאמר"; see *Malbim* and *Mishbetzos Zahav* ad loc.).[14]

Yehoshua showed Bnei Yisrael that great spiritual heights could be attained and that the Torah would continue to thrive even in Moshe's absence. Yehoshua was the first person to accept the Torah from another human and then spread its instruction further (see *Avos* 1:1). He was similarly the first person to receive *semichah* (colloquially translated as "Rabbinic ordination") and to inherit the "kingship" from a previous "king" (see *Rambam, Hilchos*

---

13. Even prior to Yehoshua's reign, Hashem assured Moshe that Yehoshua (like Moshe himself; see footnote 6 above) possessed the ability to connect with each individual member of Bnei Yisrael and to guide each person according to his unique character and capabilities (see *Rashi, Bamidbar* 27:18). *Sefer HaZikaron LeMaran HaGri"i Frankel* (pp. 229–30) records a similar idea, explaining why Yehoshua, rather than Pinchas, was chosen as the leader; see there.

Nonetheless, Yehoshua also possessed the ability to separate himself from the nation when necessary — to take a strong, even unpopular, stance when deemed worthy. See *Chafetz Chaim* (*Shemiras HaLashon*, vol. 2, note to ch. 19) who explains that Yehoshua and Calev took different approaches to leadership in this regard. See also *Sefer HaZikaron* (ibid.).

14. *Ze'ev Yitrof* (*Nevi'im Rishonim*, ch. 30) notes another parallel between Yehoshua's and Moshe's reigns. *Chazal* write (*Bamidbar Rabbah* 22:6) that if not for Yehoshua's miscalculation that cost him ten years of his life (see our comments to *Perakim* 22–24, fn. 8, for delineation of his error), Yehoshua would have lived for 120 years, like Moshe. *Ze'ev Yitrof* further points to Rashi's comment (*Devarim* 31:29) that Moshe considered himself to be "alive" throughout Yehoshua's lifetime. Also interesting is that Hashem granted both Yehoshua and Moshe "control" over nature, allowing each of them to halt the sun's path (see *Rashi, Shemos* 17:12; *Yehoshua* 10:12–14).

Sanhedrin 4:1 and *Hilchos Melachim* 1:3).[15] In a sense, Yehoshua established the power of the *mesorah* (Torah tradition) and enabled it to flourish in all post-Sinai generations.[16]

Nonetheless, we will later see that Bnei Yisrael never *completely* appreciated Yehoshua (see our comments on *Perakim* 22–24). As much as Yehoshua tried, replacing Moshe proved impossible. The Jewish people did not entirely come to terms with Moshe's absence, nor with the fact that *no* leader could ever entirely take his place. Their inability to fully accept and respect Yehoshua had adverse lasting consequences, which became most evident toward the end of Yehoshua's reign (as will be described in our comments on the final *Perakim* of the *Sefer*).

---

15. Many sources indicate that Moshe and Yehoshua were not literally "kings" with all the ramifications of that title. See *Nachalas Shimon* (*Sefer Shoftim*, ch. 1, specifically 1:8), who expounds on this point and lists a number of differences between literal "kingship" and other forms of leadership.

For further discussion regarding the precise status of the rule of Moshe and Yehoshua, see *Nachalas Shimon* (*Sefer Yehoshua*, ch. 6, fn. 7; *Sefer Shoftim* 24:4); *Sha'ar HaMelech* (by R. Chaim Kanievsky *shlita*, p. 7). See also my comments in *Toras HaKavod* (ch. 7, sec. 3).

16. R. Yitzchak Volozhiner (son of R. Chaim Volozhiner, note on his father's famous work, *Ruach Chaim*, Avos 1:1, p. 22 in R. Goldberg ed.) adds that, whereas no other Jew could even hope to understand the Torah as well as Moshe, Yehoshua's level of comprehension served as a model toward which the masses could strive. The average Jew could not dream of paralleling the "sun" (Moshe); they could try, however, to *reflect* the Torah's light (like the moon, represented by Yehoshua) through tireless effort.

PERAKIM 5–8:

A New Land;
A New Mission

FTER INAUGURATING YEHOSHUA AS their new leader, Bnei Yisrael were ready to launch the next phase in pursuit of their destiny to establish themselves as a wholly sanctified nation in Eretz Yisrael. As mentioned in our opening comments to *Perakim* 1–4, the Jewish people, upon entering their Promised Land, were presented with unprecedented challenges. Yet, these very challenges, somewhat paradoxically, offered fresh spiritual opportunities.

Spirituality in a Natural World

THROUGHOUT THEIR SOJOURN in the desert, Bnei Yisrael basked in the manifest guidance and care of the Almighty, who personally shepherded them, physically and spiritually, for forty years. That Guiding Hand retreated backstage when Bnei Yisrael crossed the Jordan River. After a full generation of gradual national maturation, the Jews entering Eretz Yisrael would be expected both to tend to their own physical needs and to take more spiritual initiative than their forebears. The impetus for spiritual growth would have to stem from the people, rather than from

Above.[1] As we described in our opening remarks to *Perakim* 1–4, even the very nature of Torah study changed when the Jews reached Eretz Yisrael. In lieu of lessons packaged neatly and delivered directly by God, Torah study would become a human initiative, driven by and driving the inculcation of Divine thought and values.

Accordingly, as Bnei Yisrael advanced into their national homeland, Divine Providence saw to it that the *mann*, an icon of the previous era, become depleted (see 5:12; *Metzudos David* and *Radak* ad loc.). The *mann* served a dual function. Most simply, it was a readily available meal through which the Jews of the desert nourished themselves with little effort. More essentially, it contained unique spiritual qualities that nurtured Bnei Yisrael's souls.[2] Its disappearance marked a monumental shift in the relationship between Hashem and Bnei Yisrael. Hashem would no longer spoon-feed His flock material and spiritual sustenance like a mother providing for her helpless young. Rather, Bnei Yisrael would be expected to provide — both materially and spiritually — for themselves.[3]

---

1. Although the previous generation, the *dor de'ah* ("generation of knowledge"; see *Vayikra Rabbah* 9:1), certainly displayed tremendous faith in Hashem — by following Him out of Egypt, crossing the *Yam Suf*, accepting the Torah with the famous phrase "נעשה ונשמע" ("we will do and we will listen"), and traversing the desert with sole reliance on the One Above (see *Yirmeyahu* 2:2) — nevertheless, that generation did not face the challenge of creating spirituality on its own. They are forever lauded for their faith in and closeness to Hashem, but it was those who entered Eretz Yisrael who were required to establish such a sublime existence from the ground up.

2. See *Ramban* (*Shemos* 16:6) and *Rabbeinu Bachya* (*Shemos* 16:4) who elaborate on this point. For further discussion of the concept of food acting as "spiritual nourishment," see *Kisvei Rabbeinu Bachya* (*Shulchan shel Arba, Sha'ar* 4, pp. 505–6); *Maharal* (*Gur Aryeh, Bereishis* 1:21); *Sheivet Mussar* (ch. 26). See also my comments in *Toras HaKavod* (ch. 42).

3. Certainly, proper inculcation of the Torah necessitates a profound appreciation that all human accomplishment is nothing more than utilization of God's constant provision of life, sustenance, talent, etc. Nonetheless, from this point onward, the Jews would need to exert more effort to care for themselves and their souls.

More profoundly yet, the Jews would be charged to suffuse ordinary, earthly pursuits with spiritual meaning. They would need to infuse holiness into all mundane undertakings — to wage wars, till the earth, build homes, establish social structures, etc. — all through the prism of the Torah's wisdom, and all with the goal of creating a society that reflects and radiates the beauty and brilliance of the Torah. In the words of the Malbim (in a different context; see *Sefer HaCarmel*, s.v. 'גוף ולבוש וכו),[i] the Jews were charged to "plow, seed, winnow, and sift in order to separate the fruit from its scrap, and to 'raise the spiritual spark' [from within the food] toward holiness."4

This new responsibility was obviously far more demanding than their previous way of life in the desert. *Chazal* record (*Yalkut Shimoni* #7) that Bnei Yisrael were told to repent before entering Eretz Yisrael and eating the fruits of the land. *Mishbetzos Zahav* (p. 101) explains that to prepare and eat regular food with the

---

4. The Malbim explains that this task represents mankind's principal mission since Adam HaRishon's sin. Before man sinned, all creation was perfect; Divine holiness emanated openly from all things. Adam's sin jumbled good and evil. Since that moment, man's job has been to sift the good from the bad within creation and to reveal, through his own efforts ("בזעת אפיך" — *Bereishis* 3:19), the hidden holiness latent in all objects and activities.

In the desert, guided by the Divine hand, the Jews were minimally engaged in this global task. Upon entering Eretz Yisrael, however, this mandate once again applied in full force.

According to R. Dessler *zt"l*, man is charged with a more profound assignment yet. R. Dessler (*Michtav Me'Eliyahu*, vol. 1, pp. 304–12) explains that physical objects and pursuits exist only on "low planes" of spiritual cognizance. One who matures recognizes "worlds of truer existence"; he views the *spiritual realm* as reality and the *physical world* as a mere tool, or even as a façade of sorts. (For more elaboration on this idea, see *Michtav Me'Eliyahu*, vol. 1, p. 178, s.v. אבל and p. 276, s.v. לפי, where R. Dessler explains the essence of "nature" and man's role in the world.) Accordingly, the Jews were challenged not only to suffuse the physical with spirituality, but to perform an even more impressive feat: to transcend their perception of physicality even while partaking routinely in the mundane activities of life.

same degree of holiness with which the *mann* was gathered and consumed requires tremendous spiritual strength. Bnei Yisrael were charged, paradoxically, to achieve loftier spiritual heights than they had reached in the desert, all while living in a world in which God's daily assistance was less manifest.[5] They would need to cultivate their characters to the point that Godliness would emanate from their own efforts. In a sense, they would need to inject Hashem into daily life, as Hashem would no longer do it for them. So daunting was this task that Rashi comments (5:12) that had they been afforded the opportunity, Bnei Yisrael would have chosen to continue eating *mann* rather than undertake the new challenge. And in fact, according to a number of commentators, it was anxiety over this anticipated transition that motivated the spies' discouraging report following their mission to Eretz Yisrael roughly forty years prior, a cataclysm that delayed Bnei Yisrael's arrival in their homeland by decades.[6]

---

5. The two sides of this paradox can further be understood by analyzing a *Tannaic* dispute (recorded in *Chullin* 16b–17a) regarding another change in Bnei Yisrael's dietary habits after entering Eretz Yisrael. On one hand, R. Yishmael states that the Jewish people, while sojourning in the desert, were prohibited from eating wildlife for physical delight alone; all animals (that were suitable for *korbanos*) had to be offered to Hashem before dining on their meat. Upon entering Eretz Yisrael, however, Bnei Yisrael were permitted to consume even meat that was not offered as a *korban*. Commentators explain (see *Sfas Emes, Re'eh* 12:20, year 5649) that the Jewish people, upon entering Eretz Yisrael, had the ability to partake in such mundane activity with a new sense of holiness. On the other hand, however, R. Akiva opines that Bnei Yisrael, while under Hashem's close watch in the desert, were permitted to eat meat even without slaughtering it properly. Only upon entering Eretz Yisrael did the Jewish people need to be ever more careful to suffuse their food and its preparation with holiness. (I thank R. Yitzchak Salid for directing me to this point.)

6. *Nesivos Shalom* (*Shelach*, pp. 66–7) explains that the spies were afraid that the need to engage the physical world and depend upon human initiative would jeopardize the lofty spiritual status they enjoyed in the desert. Their reference to the "giants" who inhabited the land was, in truth, an expression of their trepidation

Yet, willing or not, eager or not, Bnei Yisrael had little choice but to accept this mission.[7] And in truth, they had much help from their surroundings. The challenges outlined in the pages of this chapter notwithstanding, Eretz Yisrael was, is, and will always be the most ideal place to achieve the highest levels of sanctity.[8] It is a land where the Divine Presence dwells more palpably than in any other place on Earth.[9] As long as they would

---

about this formidable task. Similarly, Maharal (*Chiddushei Aggados, Sotah* 34b) writes that the spies feared living in Eretz Yisrael because they were accustomed to the miraculous nature of their existence in the desert, and they were apprehensive about entering a land in which they would be limited by the confines of nature.

7. The Ibn Ezra (*Shemos* 14:13) writes that the previous generation did not possess the boldness necessary to conquer Eretz Yisrael. Having served as slaves, their mentality was characterized by a degree of fear and meekness, unfit for years of confrontation and battle. The current generation, on the other hand, although they shared some fears expressed by their ancestors (as described above), was ready for this challenge.

8. Serving God in Eretz Yisrael constitutes the highest form of service, exceptionally more elevated than service of Hashem in the Diaspora (see *Ramban, Bereishis* 26:5; *Vayikra* 18:25). In fact, the entire Torah can be read as a guide toward this ultimate service. Rashi (*Bereishis* 1:1) famously comments that the Torah begins by providing proof of our nation's claim to Eretz Yisrael. The rest of the Torah can be read as a log of Bnei Yisrael's journey toward the holy land. The Torah concludes with Bnei Yisrael on the brink of entering Eretz Yisrael, connoting that it is upon *us*, the adherents of the Torah, to follow the Torah's directives and bring this idyllic existence to fruition. (See also *Gur Aryeh, Bereishis* 1:1.)

9. The Torah stresses that Eretz Yisrael belongs to Hashem; its inhabitants are mere tenants (see *Vayikra* 25:23 with *Seforno*). *Nesivos Shalom* (*Shelach*, p. 63) explains that life in Eretz Yisrael is governed by Hashem's "direct hand" and exists on a supernatural plane. (Yet, as opposed to Hashem's manifest assistance while Bnei Yisrael journeyed through the desert, in Eretz Yisrael, Hashem began to mask His "hand" behind the laws of nature, as mentioned above.) See *Nachalas Shimon* (ch. 45) for an extensive list of statements of *Chazal* and commentators regarding Eretz Yisrael's elevated status and its positive impact upon the people who live there. Interestingly, *Nesivos Shalom* (ibid.) writes that part of the error of the spies (during Moshe's reign) was that they saw only the *challenges* of life in Eretz Yisrael, but they were blind to the supernatural qualities of the land that would *assist* their efforts.

utilize this opportunity to its fullest, the sacredness of their new home would have transformative ramifications for the Jewish people.

New Communality and Reinforced Commitment

IN FACT, THE generation crossing into Eretz Yisrael comprised a "new nation" of sorts, as Eretz Yisrael confers special status upon its inhabitants. *Chazal* state (*Horayos* 3a) that only Jews who reside in Eretz Yisrael are considered part of the *kahal* — the unified group of Bnei Yisrael. Similarly, the *Zohar* (*Emor*, vol. 3, p. 93) asserts that the Jewish people are referred to as "one nation" (גוי אחד) only in Eretz Yisrael. The Maharal (*Nesivos Olam*, vol. 1, *Nesiv HaTzedakah*, ch. 6, p. 182) seconds this point.[ii] Likewise, the Rogatchover Gaon (*Tzafnas Pane'ach, Shemos*, ch. 13, p. 61) writes that Bnei Yisrael became an "eternal community" only upon entering Eretz Yisrael.[iii]

Accordingly, commentators note (see *Maharal* ibid.; *Beis Yishai, Derashos* p. 27) that from the instant Bnei Yisrael entered their land, each member of the nation became responsible for the choices of his fellow (*Sanhedrin* 43b: כל ישראל ערבים זה בזה — "Each Jew is a guarantor for his fellow").[10] Although Bnei Yisrael were certainly required to care for one another even prior to entering Eretz Yisrael, the Jewish people became a complete, cohesive unit only upon entering their land.[11] Many commentators

---

10. The Gemara implies that Bnei Yisrael first accepted this principle even while still crossing the Yarden. (See also *Nachalas Shimon*, ch. 12, and *Posei'ach Sha'ar*, Sanhedrin 43b, pp. 916–7.)

11. The dictum of *areivus* — mutual accountability — carries a number of practical ramifications: the obligation to sense a companion's need for help (see *Mishbetzos Zahav*, p. 347); the obligation to verbally dissuade and even physically deter another from sinning (see *Metzudos David* 7:12; *Rabbeinu Yonah, Meiri*, and *Maharsha* on

explain (see *Mishbetzos Zahav*, pp. 128–9) that this status of guarantors is based on the idea that Bnei Yisrael are considered one conjoined body. This sublime unified body constitutes a level of spiritual existence exceedingly greater than that of its individual parts, as described by R. Shlomo Fisher *shlita* (*Beis Yishai, Derashos*, p. 121):[iv]

> The sacred Torah is not the Torah of the *individual*, but the Torah of the *klal* — that is, of the whole Jewish nation. This is indeed an amazing concept. An entire nation — men, women, and children, wise and foolish alike — together comprise a holy people, and each individual Jew constitutes a limb of the entirety of *Kenesses Yisrael* (the Congregation of Israel), which represents the Divine Presence[12]... The true purpose and essence of the *mitzvos* is realized only [when the *mitzvos* are practiced] by the community at large.[13]

Hence, Bnei Yisrael, as this cohesive nation with a more mature spiritual mission, were positioned to achieve wondrous levels of spirituality. To initiate and properly direct their profound undertaking, the Jewish people needed to reaffirm their "*kedushas*

Sanhedrin 43b); the ability to fulfill a fellow's ritual responsibilities through one's own actions (see *Rosh Hashanah* 29a with *Rashi* s.v. אע״פ). The underlying precept is clear: the Jewish nation is one unified mass, and each individual plays a part in that transcendent unit.

12. R. Hutner *zt"l* (*Pachad Yitzchak, Pesach* #33) likewise explains that *Kenesses Yisrael* is not merely the conglomerate of individual Jews; rather, it is a sublime entity of which all individual Jews are part.[v]

For further elaboration on the concept of "*Kenesses Yisrael*" as the entirety of the Jewish nation and as a representation of the Divine Presence, see *Maharal* (*Gur Aryeh, Vayikra* 20:3; R. Hartman's footnotes ad loc. 33–44). See also *Ma'ayan Beis HaSho'evah* (*Shemos* 13:8).

13. There are even some *mitzvos* that are incumbent upon the nation at large, rather than upon each individual alone (see Rambam, *Sefer HaMitzvos*, end of positive commandments, s.v. וכששתתכל כל אלו). See also Rabbeinu Avraham ben HaRambam (*HaMaspik L'Ovdei Hashem*, ch. 1) who explains that while the *mitzvos* of the Torah are directed at the masses, individuals can rise above the basic requirements.

Yisrael" (exclusive sanctity of the Jew) — on both individual and national levels. To this end, Hashem commanded and arranged that they attend immediately to the following essential *mitzvos*:

A) *Bris milah*: Upon arriving in Eretz Yisrael, all uncircumcised men immediately underwent circumcision (5:2–3). The *Navi* remarks that this event constituted Bnei Yisrael's "second" *bris milah*. Rashi (along with most commentators) explains that this episode marked the second mass national circumcision, the first one being when they left Egypt. By designating this event as the "second" in a series, the *Navi* implies that this occasion was tantamount to that pivotal juncture when Bnei Yisrael were first forged as a united people with a united purpose. Just as they required the first national *bris milah* to solidify their covenant with Hashem as a newly liberated people, so too they required this second *bris milah* to imbue their current experience with a revitalized commitment to Hashem.[14]

Furthermore, a *bris milah* is one of the essential components of Jewish conversion. As recited at the *bris* of every Jewish boy, it represents "inducting the child into the covenant of Avraham Avinu." When Bnei Yisrael entered Eretz Yisrael, they underwent a "conversion" of sorts, as they did when they left Egypt and received the Torah (see *Kereisos* 9a that *bris milah* was an indispensable component of the "conversion" at Har Sinai).[15]

---

14. Interestingly, the Ralbag (5:2) comments that even the original *bris milah* (when Bnei Yisrael left Egypt) was performed in anticipation of entering Eretz Yisrael. It is entering Eretz Yisrael, and all that this monumental step implies, that most necessitates this covenant.

15. Rashi (5:2, based on *Yevamos* 71b) offers an additional interpretation of the term "second" in the *pasuk* in question. Unlike the *bris milah* performed in Egypt, the one performed in Eretz Yisrael included *"periyah,"* the "second" element of *bris*

B) *Korban Pesach*: After the communal *bris milah*, Bnei Yisrael brought a *Korban Pesach* (5:10), once again reminiscent of the Exodus from Egypt, when the Jews were first forged as a nation.[16] Offering this *korban* in Egypt represented an unwavering commitment to Hashem (because sacrificing sheep would have resulted in capital punishment at the hands of the Egyptians had God not taken Bnei Yisrael out of Egypt — see *Shemos* 8:22; *Shemos Rabbah* 16:3). Likewise, the *Korban Pesach* offered in Yehoshua's time represented the Jews' personal and national submission to Hashem's leadership at that seminal juncture.

    Korban Pesach is likened to the aforementioned mitzvah of *bris milah*, as both affirm commitment to our nation's eternal covenant. *Korban Pesach* and *bris milah* are the only two *mitzvos aseh* (positive commandments) that bear the harsh punishment of *kareis* for one who neglects them. *Kareis* literally means being "severed" from the nation, a fitting consequence for neglecting these *mitzvos* that symbolize our national identity and our mission as emissaries of God. There is also a specific prohibition for an uncircumcised male to partake of the *Korban Pesach* (see *Shemos* 12:48; *Sefer HaChinuch* #17). Reneging on the charge of the *bris milah* perforce cuts a person off from the mission symbolized by the *Korban Pesach*. *Chazal* (*Mechilta, Shemos* ibid.,

---

milah, meant to further expose the spot of circumcision. *Mishbetzos Zahav* (p. 84) explains that Bnei Yisrael in Eretz Yisrael would have greater opportunity to "expose" the glory of our nation. (For more on the halachic possibility of undergoing *milah* without *periyah*, see *Nachalas Shimon*, ch. 14.)

16. R. Moshe David Valle *zt"l* (cited in *Mishbetzos Zahav*, p. 95) notes that Bnei Yisrael entered Eretz Yisrael on the tenth of Nissan (see 4:19), the same date on which the Jews first took the sheep in Egypt (to ready them for slaughter). R. Shlomo Fisher (*Beis Yishai, Derashos* p. 29) elaborates on this point further.

Bo #15) even intimate that *Korban Pesach,* like *bris milah,* represents an aspect of *conversion!* It is not surprising, then, that *Korban Pesach* was chosen as the proper measure to reaffirm the Jewish people's national calling upon on their arrival in Eretz Yisrael.[17]

The symbolic significance of the timing of this *Korban Pesach* is uniquely evident according to the opinions that the Biblical obligation to offer an annual *Korban Pesach* first took effect only once Bnei Yisrael arrived in Eretz Yisrael (see *Rashi, Shemos* 12:25, based on *Mechilta*).[18] Apparently, Bnei Yisrael were not a wholly constituted nation until they arrived in their land, and the function of the *Korban Pesach* did not fully apply to them until such time.

Tosafos (*Kiddushin* 37b s.v. הואיל) write that the requirement to offer a *Korban Pesach* annually may have taken effect only after the people had *fully* settled the land (i.e., after *yerushah v'yeshivah,* a number of years after the Jews' initial arrival).[19] Yet, Hashem commanded Bnei

---

17. The idea that the *Korban Pesach* highlights the Jewish identity of those who offer it is evident from a plethora of other *halachos* and comments of *Chazal.* For instance, one may not allow an apostate or non-Jew to partake in the *Korban Pesach* (*Shemos* 12:43, 45; *Sefer HaChinuch* #13–4). In addition, the *Korban Pesach,* even though it is offered by every *individual,* possesses some characteristics of a *"communal* sacrifice," as it symbolizes one's association with the Jewish community at large (see *Teshuvos Avnei Nezer, Orach Chaim* 538:5, 9; *Kehillos Yaakov, Yoma* 2:2). See R. Michael Rosensweig *shlita's* essay (printed in "Pesach-to-Go," 5774, pp. 34–42) for elaboration on these and additional points. R. Hutner (*Pachad Yitzchak, Pesach* #33) echoes these ideas: "Just as the Redemption from Egypt created the concept of *Tzibbur Yisrael* (the community of Jews), so does the *Korban Pesach* generate the designation of *tzibbur* (community) among the group that offers it."[vi]

18. See *Nachalas Shimon* (ch. 15) for a fuller discussion regarding whether the obligation to offer the *Korban Pesach* applied throughout Bnei Yisrael's stay in the desert or only once they arrived in Eretz Yisrael.

19. See our comments on *Perakim* 13–21 regarding other *mitzvos* that applied

Yisrael to offer the *Korban Pesach* that first year, seemingly to symbolize the profound crystallization of national identity that characterized their arrival in Eretz Yisrael.[20]

C) *Kabbalas HaTorah*: According to *Chazal's* tradition of the chronology of events (as recorded in *Seder Olam*, ch. 11; *Sotah* 36a; *Rashi* and *Radak* 8:30), even before performing the *bris milah* and offering the *Korban Pesach*, Bnei Yisrael ascended *Har Gerizim* and *Har Eival* to renew their vows to follow the Torah (see *pesukim* 8:30–35).[21] As Bnei Yisrael became a qualitatively more mature entity upon crossing the Jordan River, it was only sensible that they undergo this formal reacceptance of the Torah.[22]

---

only after Bnei Yisrael settled the land.

20. See *Meshech Chochmah* (*Bamidbar* 9:7, cited in *Nachalas Shimon*, ch. 15, fn. 1) who offers a slightly different reason as to why Hashem instructed Bnei Yisrael to offer a special *Korban Pesach* at that time.

21. One opinion in *Chazal*, however, maintains that Bnei Yisrael accepted the *mitzvos* at *Har Gerizim* and *Har Eival* fourteen years later, after conquering and settling the land (see *Yerushalmi Sotah* 7:3 and *Nachalas Shimon* 10:4).

22. The Ramban (intro. to *Devarim*) posits that many *mitzvos* did not apply *at all* until the Jewish people entered Eretz Yisrael! Accordingly, this event did not represent a mere "reacceptance" of the Torah; it was, in a sense, an inauguration. (Other commentators, however, disagree with the Ramban; see *Abarbanel*, intro. to *Devarim*, s.v. ואמנם הכונה; *Shu"t Radvaz*, vol. 6 #2143.)

The commentators dispute exactly which parts of the Torah were written down on the stones and reviewed at this event. Options include: the entire Torah; *Sefer Devarim*; a list of the *mitzvos*; the Ten Commandments. See *Nachalas Shimon* (34:2). See also *Ze'ev Yitrof* (*Shavuos*, ch. 75) who explicates the profound meaning inherent in recording various aspects of the Torah on these stones.

The Spiritual Challenges of War

IN THE WAKE of these well-timed and highly symbolic *mitzvos*, Yehoshua encouraged his people to suffuse each of their military campaigns and civil endeavors with sanctity. In their first battle (the battle of Yericho), Yehoshua aimed to do so to an extreme. Commentators explain (see *Mishbetzos Zahav*, p. 111; *Nachalas Shimon*, end of ch. 24) that the purpose of encircling Yericho was to surround the city with immense holiness and thereby weed out the foul impurities that had been brewing among its inhabitants.[23] Yehoshua instructed that all spoils be consecrated to the Almighty, emphasizing, from the outset, that the conquest of Eretz Yisrael had a higher purpose.[24] Indeed, *Chazal* (*Yalkut Shimoni* #15; see *Radak* 6:17) define Yehoshua's sanctification of the spoils as a form of "tithe" to Hashem. In a similar vein, tradition has it (see *Rashi* 6:15–17) that the seventh and final circuit of the seven-day siege took place on Shabbos, the day that the presence of the Almighty most permeates Earth.[25]

---

23. Commentaries explain that it was these impurities that motivated Yehoshua to forbid future generations from rebuilding Yericho (6:26); see *Ralbag* (6:17) and R. Moshe David Valle's comments cited in *Mishbetzos Zahav* (p. 123). (Regarding the permissibility of building Yericho today, see *Teshuvos Tzitz Eliezer*, vol. 10, 1:12, pp. 29–30; *Nachalas Shimon*, ch. 26.)

24. Rabbeinu Avraham ben HaRambam (cited in *Nachalas Shimon* 24:4) adds that Yehoshua intended to teach his people to refrain from unnecessary physical pleasures. See also *Sefer HaChinuch* (#505) for an additional moral reason why one would refrain from enjoying the spoils of a defeated enemy. Some commentators explain, however, that Yehoshua understood that Bnei Yisrael did not deserve the spoils since the war against Yericho was won in a supernatural, miraculous fashion, and the spoils therefore belonged fully to Hashem (see *Nachalas Shimon* ibid.).

25. Interestingly, some note (see R. David Avraham's *Hei'ir Mi'Mizrach — Hoshanos*, p. 37) that this tradition is recalled each year on *Hoshana Rabbah*, when it is customary to recite the "Song of Shabbos" and encircle the *bimah* seven

Yet, in the process of internalizing and fulfilling these lessons and goals, Bnei Yisrael encountered some devastating setbacks. *Chazal* comment that Yehoshua made a few slight, yet significant, miscalculations. Preoccupied with the lofty spiritual potential of his military campaign, he lost sight of Bnei Yisrael's broader mission of affirming their faithfulness to Hashem through everyday *mitzvos* and mundane activity. *Chazal* explain (*Eruvin* 63b; *Megillah* 3a) that the angel that approached Yehoshua before the battle of Yericho (5:13–15) came to warn him of this very pitfall. The angel scolded Yehoshua for being remiss in neglecting:

a) the *Korban Tamid*, the sacrifice offered twice daily, which serves as a staple of religious life;

b) Torah study, which is meant to be central to one's daily routine;

c) procreation, the basis of family life and the guarantor of the nation's future.

But Yehoshua did not fully appreciate the angel's warning. He thought that the angel's mission was merely to assist him in battle (see *Rashi* 5:14; *Radak* 6:2). In actuality, though, the angel's goal was to *rebuke* him and to redirect his attention to the basics — ensuring that holiness pervades daily life — before focusing on spreading that holiness to conquered towns.[26]

---

times, reminiscent of the battle of Yericho. The "Song of Shabbos" also makes reference to the horn of a "*re'em*," which serves as the symbol of Yehoshua's strength and glory (see *Rashi, Devarim* 33:17), and alludes to the *shofar* blown during this battle. (For a halachic discussion regarding which wars are permitted on Shabbos, see *Nachalas Shimon*, ch. 23.)

26. For further explanation of *Chazal*'s comments regarding the angel's message, Yehoshua's response, and Yehoshua's reaction after the defeat at Ay, see *Merchavim* (vol. 3, pp. 71–74; 77–80).

It should be noted that *Chazal*'s interpretation of the angel's message (which

Chazal (*Sanhedrin* 44a; *Rashi* 7:10) add that Yehoshua's insistence that Bnei Yisrael consecrate all spoils of Yericho was similarly miscalculated. Although his reasoning was sound and his sentiments would have been well placed in an ideal setting,[27] Yehoshua should have realized the difficulty involved in forgoing the booty and that Bnei Yisrael were not yet ready for such standards.[28] The

---

focuses on Bnei Yisrael's failure to uphold various *mitzvos*) is not readily apparent from the text of the *Navi*. A number of classic commentators indeed struggle to fit *Chazal's* reading into the *pesukim* (see *Radak* 5:14; *Nachalas Shimon*, ch. 20). Nonetheless, after scrutinizing the stories that *are* in fact clear in the text, one begins to appreciate the textual allusions to *Chazal's* tradition. Firstly, the very visit of an angel indicates that a *significant* message was delivered, one that is more consequential than is evident from a cursory read of the story. Furthermore, Achan's sin (described below), and the fact that Bnei Yisrael were held accountable for it, reflected imperfections in the personal characters of the nation at large, as will be explained shortly. It is sensible, therefore, that Bnei Yisrael would receive *some* Divine message (such as by means of an angel) to direct them. Also noteworthy is the fact that Yehoshua was told to remove his shoes at this point (5:15). This directive parallels the command for Moshe to remove his shoes when he encountered the burning bush (*Shemos* 3:5), a meeting that proved to be one of the most crucial junctures in history. Indeed, according to *Chazal's* tradition, the angel was calling Yehoshua to leadership, similar to Hashem's call to Moshe at the burning bush.

27. *Chazal* write (*Yerushalmi Berachos* 9:5; *Tanchuma, Vayechi* #8) that Hashem "agreed" that Yehoshua's consecration of the spoils was essentially a good initiative. (See also *Nachalas Shimon* 24:4 and addition #1; *Maharatz Chayes, Sanhedrin* 44a s.v. קום.) In fact, Moshe Rabbeinu consecrated spoils of war (see *Bamidbar* 21:2 with *Rashi*).

28. The *Shiyarei Korban* (*Yerushalmi Sanhedrin* 27b s.v. עוד ולא) notes that Hashem even allowed Bnei Yisrael to eat non-kosher food during those years of war (see *Chullin* 17a). Surely, to prohibit generally permitted indulgences was inappropriate at that time.

[As for the reason behind the unique allowance to consume non-kosher food, the Rambam (*Hilchos Melachim* 8:1) writes that permission was granted only insofar as the pressures of war demanded. The Rambam (ibid. 8:2) and *Ya'avetz* (cited in R. Chavel's footnotes to R. Bachya, *Devarim* 6:11) liken this law to the distinctive halachah of "*eishes yefas to'ar*" (female captive; see *Devarim* 21:10–14). *Chazal* write (*Kiddushin* 21b) that the Torah, appreciating the

focus on sanctifying the spoils also diverted the people from their most essential goal — inculcating the directives and messages of the Torah into their daily endeavors, as stated above.

Correspondingly, *Chazal* record that Hashem rebuked Yehoshua for not personally joining his people in the war with Ay (see *Rashi* and *Mishbetzos Zahav* 7:10). Hashem was teaching Yehoshua that if he was to succeed in guiding the nation toward their central, overarching mission, he could not simply *instruct*; he would need to *personally model* Godly living.[29]

---

challenges of wartime, granted soldiers special permission to marry non-Jewish captives (for detailed laws, see *Rambam* ibid.; *Sefer HaChinuch* #532). *Chazal* stress, however, that capitalizing on this situational dispensation is certainly less than ideal and will often spur tragic repercussions (see *Rashi, Devarim* 21:11; *Sanhedrin* 107a).

The Ramban and R. Bachya (*Devarim* 6:11), in contradistinction to the *Rambam* cited above, opine that soldiers, during wartime, were permitted to partake of non-kosher food even when kosher food was readily available. The *Meshech Chochmah* and *Ha'Amek Davar* (*Devarim* ad loc.) note, however, that since non-kosher food could sully one's heart (spiritually), the Torah (ibid. 6:12) cautions soldiers not to let this behavior have lasting effects on their personalities and sensibilities.

The *Panim Yafos* (*Devarim* 6:10) adds that Bnei Yisrael, during their holy conquest, had the opportunity to extract and expose a sanctity that is generally inaccessible, buried (metaphysically) deep inside non-kosher food. They were therefore permitted to consume, during that era, victuals prohibited in any other setting.]

29. Yehoshua certainly did not lack deep care and concern for his people. Indeed, Yehoshua argued with Hashem Himself in defense of his people after they were punished at Ay (see 7:7–9; *Rashi* and *Mishbetzos Zahav* 7:23). Nonetheless, Yehoshua did not initially grasp the need for the leader's full, active involvement with his people.

In truth, even Moshe Rabbeinu made this mistake. *Chazal* comment (*Mechilta*, cited in *Rashi, Shemos* 17:12) that Moshe was incorrect for sending his people to battle Amalek while he prayed for the nation from afar. Although he intended to help them through his prayer (and he did!), nevertheless, it would have been more proper for him to physically lead his people onto the battlefield. Yehoshua seemingly made the same mistake. He certainly did not callously send his men to

These misjudgments by Yehoshua led to a tragic error by the nation at large. While focused on grand objectives of spreading holiness and ridding the land of impurities, many among Bnei Yisrael apparently overlooked imperfections in their personal characters. Achan infamously disobeyed Yehoshua's command and looted spoils from Yericho, and the entire nation was held accountable and suffered for his transgression (see the sharp language of the *Navi* — 7:11). R. Eliyahu Dessler *zt"l* (*Michtav Me'Eliyahu*, vol. 1, p. 162)[vii] explains that general laxity of the masses regarding any given transgressions allows dissidents to view those evils as viable options and to eventually perpetrate them. Had all individuals been duly appalled by the mere thought of misappropriating consecrated items, and had their disapproval been apparent from their every action and disposition, Achan would never have been so brazen as to commit such a crime. Sins of individuals are not committed in a vacuum; each member of the nation at large shares responsibility.[30]

This calamity also illustrated a gap in Bnei Yisrael's unity. As elaborated above, Bnei Yisrael, when representing a singular cohesive body, can attain the loftiest of spiritual heights. In this tragic

---

war while he took refuge at home. Rather, he thought that it was proper to assist on the spiritual front while his army fought physically. Yet, he, like Moshe, apparently miscalculated.

30. Commentators debate how to precisely define Achan's infraction and how to justify the death penalty prescribed him. Some explain that he violated the law of *cheirem* (an executive consecration invoked under extenuating circumstances by a national leader or leaders). Others opine that he was guilty of insurrection against Yehoshua, the leader and prophet. Other commentators contend that he desecrated Shabbos. (For elaboration, see *Nachalas Shimon*, ch. 27.)

Chazal (*Sanhedrin* 44a) add that Achan transgressed the *entire* Torah. They also enumerate some particularly heinous crimes that he committed (reversing his circumcision; adultery). Seemingly, *Chazal* understand the sin recorded by the *Navi* to be indicative of a more far-reaching epidemic. (See also *Maharal, Chiddushei Aggados, Sanhedrin* ad loc.)

episode, however, Bnei Yisrael failed to rebuke the perpetrator and thereby uplift one another (see *Sanhedrin* 43b–44a).[31] Fittingly, the nation was punished collectively, as a single unit, as Hashem taught them that to accomplish their mission, they must remain completely unified and responsible for one another.[32]

Recovery... With Some Lasting Consequences

THE JEWISH PEOPLE learned from their mistakes, and Yehoshua made the necessary adjustments. First, Yehoshua publicly punished Achan (7:24–25),[33] the direct perpetrator of the evil. He also made sure to become more involved with his people and to direct them first-hand. To this end, he personally led the charge

---

31. The Gemara records a dispute as to whether or not Hashem punishes the Jewish nation in its entirety for sins committed covertly by individuals (*nistaros*). Many commentators conclude that the general populace is punished only when it knows about the wrongdoing and is remiss in preventing or reacting to it (see *Posei'ach Sha'ar, Sanhedrin* ad loc. p. 921). The Gemara records that Achan's family (and presumably others as well; see *Meiri, Sanhedrin* ad loc.) were indeed aware of Achan's infraction but remained passive nonetheless.

It should be noted that according to R. Dessler's comments (quoted in the text), the nation at large is *always* responsible, to a degree, for an individual's infraction. The debate recorded in the Gemara should be understood as discussing *culpability*, but according to all opinions, the entire community certainly shares a degree of *responsibility*. (For additional understandings of the debate, with various nuances, see *Posei'ach Sha'ar* ibid., pp. 919–920.)

32. *Chazal* comment (*Sanhedrin* ad loc.; see *Rashi, Yehoshua* 7:20) that Achan committed a similar sin years earlier, during Bnei Yisrael's sojourn in the desert. Yet, the nation at large was punished for their fellow's crime only during this instance — once they entered this new land and this new era.

33. *Chazal* (cited in *Mishbetzos Zahav*, p. 152), along with classic commentators (*Rashi; Metzudos David*), disagree as to whether Achan's family was also punished with death, or if they were merely forced to witness Achan's demise.

during the second battle with Ay (see 8:9–21). He similarly recognized his miscalculation regarding the spoils of war, and he
allowed his people to plunder the spoils during the second war
with Ay (8:2, 27). Furthermore, *Chazal* say that he heeded the
angel's instruction and focused on Torah study once again (see
Rashi 8:13).[34]

To be sure, the episode of Achan's sin had some lasting negative effects. Once Bnei Yisrael showed that they could not live up
to the lofty standards envisioned by Yehoshua, they were forced
to exist on a "lower" spiritual plane. In their second battle with
Ay (8:4–22), they had to employ complex military tactics, as they
did not merit the same clear Divine assistance that they did in
their earlier battles.[35] Noting this point, the *Kli Yakar* (6:1 s.v.

---

34. The *Navi* uses similar language in *Pesukim* 8:9 and 8:13. *Chazal* (*Megillah*
bottom of 3a; see also note of *Mesoras HaShas* there) explain *Pasuk* 8:9 as referring to Yehoshua's delving into Torah study, but Rashi seemingly understands
Pasuk 8:13 as referring to this point. In truth, the two readings do not necessarily
contradict. It is quite reasonable to understand that Yehoshua heeded the angel's
teachings *completely* and spent both the night referred to in *Pasuk* 8:9 *and* the
night referred to in *Pasuk* 8:13 (as well as all other nights!) steeped in Torah study.
See also *Merchavim* (vol. 3, pp. 71–74; 77–80).

35. As described at length above, Bnei Yisrael's mission in Eretz Yisrael was to
create holiness from their *own* efforts, as opposed to relying on Heavenly assistance. Nonetheless, in the most ideal setting, their actions would have been so
pure that they would inevitably have roused the Almighty to bring about supernatural events. The *initial* effort would stem from man (i.e. אתערותא דלתתא), but
Heaven would certainly respond in kind (אתערותא דלעילא). (Commentators write
that all miracles contain at least *some* element of human initiative. See *Maharal*,
Gur Aryeh, *Bamidbar* 8:4, end of #6 in R. Hartman ed.; see also *Ramban*, *Bereishis*
6:19; R. Bachya, intro. to *Shelach*.)

It should be noted that there were definitely fantastic miracles in some of
Yehoshua's later battles (such as when the sun stopped for him; see 10:12–13).
And Bnei Yisrael's ability to win the many wars that they did was itself miraculous
(see *Tehillim* 44:4 with *Malbim* ad loc.; *Rashi*, *Yechezkel* 43:11; *Kaftor VaPherach*,
ch. 10, s.v. שעזרא גם). Nevertheless, the stark contrast between the initial battles
(the war with Yericho and the first battle with Ay) and the second war with Ay

(עוד כתבתי)[viii] adds that if not for Achan's sin, Bnei Yisrael would have conquered *all* of Eretz Yisrael almost effortlessly, as in the battle of Yericho.[36] Some commentators further maintain (see *Mishbetzos Zahav*, p. 151) that Achan's sin dampened the holiness of Bnei Yisrael's conquest to such a degree that this mishap made room for Bnei Yisrael to eventually stray and be forced into exile many years later.[37]

All things considered, Bnei Yisrael's entry into Eretz Yisrael was a tremendous success. Initially, the nation stumbled a bit in their new surroundings and with their demanding assignment, but they soon realized their profound capabilities. To signify this point, the *Navi* concludes the stories of Yericho and Ay with the national reacceptance of the Torah at *Har Gerizim* and *Har Eival*. Even though this event occurred when Bnei Yisrael first entered

---

is quite glaring, indicating a lingering impact from the episode with Achan. (But see *Ralbag* 8:1 who offers an alternate reason for the differences between the first and second battles of Ay.)

36. Accordingly, the *Kli Yakar* (ibid.) and *Malbim* (8:2) explain that Bnei Yisrael, during the second battle with Ay, were permitted to take the booty for themselves since they exerted much of their own effort in that war and therefore earned the (unfortunate) "right" to the war's spoils. It should be further noted that the loot itself did not contain the same level of holiness as the spoils from Yericho (see our comments above), and there was therefore less reason to forbid them from personal (secular) use.

37. *Mishbetzos Zahav* (p. 153) points to commentators who believe that Achan wrote the second paragraph of the *Aleinu* prayer. (The first letters of the opening words, "על כן נקוה," spell Achan's name — עכן.) Achan's sins caused Bnei Yisrael's original conquest of Eretz Yisrael to lose its intensity. He therefore composed this prayer that longs for the End of Days, when Hashem will return that heightened degree of holiness to Eretz Yisrael. (For other explanations of Achan's rationale for expropriating the booty and for composing this prayer, see *Beis Yishai*, *Derashos*, p. 209, fn. 17, s.v. והנה; R. Elchanan Shoff, *Paradise*, *Va'eschanan*, p. 201.)

[It should be noted that the Maharal seems to assume that Yehoshua, not Achan, penned *both* paragraphs of *Aleinu*; see *Be'er HaGolah*, sec. 7, s.v. חלק השלישי.]

Eretz Yisrael (according to the tradition of *Chazal*, as recorded above), the *Navi* chose to recount this episode at the conclusion of the stories of Yericho and Ay to indicate that Bnei Yisrael matured as a result of their mistakes and learned to define themselves as the new nation they had become.[38] They were now ready to proceed to the next stage of their conquest.[39]

<hr />

ENDNOTES

[i] קודם חטא אדם הראשון, היה כח השכל והרוחני ברור וצלול מבלי מבלי התערב בו שום כחות
החומה... וכמו כן היה בכל דברים הנמצאים, כי כל דבר נברא בשלמות, ולא היה צריך שום
תיקון והכשה, כי לא היה הטוב מעורב ברע כלל, והאוכל היה נקי מבלי פסולת וקליפה... אבל
אחר החטא, שנתערב טוב ורע מעץ הדעת טוב ורע, וכחות הנפשיים נתערבו ונתמזגו עם
כחות החומריים והיו לבשר וגוף אחד... נתמזג האוכל הגשמי עם כח הרוחני שבו, והיו לעצם
אחד... ומאז, זה פרי תקון החטא הקדום, לעבוד את האדמה כמו שכתוב 'בזעת אפיך תאכל'
- לחרוש ולזרוע לזרות ולהבר - כדי לברר האוכל מתוך הפסולת, ולהעלות הניצוץ הרוחני אל
הקדושה... ודבר זה יהיה נוהג עד לעתיד לבא, שאז רוח הטומאה יעבור מן הארץ, ולא יהיה
עוד צורך לעבודה ותיקון, כמו שהיה קודם החטא, כי יצא האוכל מתוקן נקי וברור - ועתיד
ארץ ישראל להוציא גלוסקאות מתוקנים בשלמותם.

[ii] כשנכנסו ישראל לארץ היו ישראל עם אחד לגמרי.

[iii] אחר שנכנסו לארץ ישראל נעשו ציבור, ונעשו מציאות אחת ניצחית.

[iv] התורה הקדושה אינה תורת הפרט, אלא תורת הכלל, דהיינו כלל האומה הישראלית.
והוא באמת ענין נפלא. שאומה שלמה - אנשים נשים וטף, חכמים וסכלים - כולם הם גוי

<hr />

38. According to the *Malbim* (8:30), the event at *Har Gerizim* and *Har Eival* actually occurred, to a degree, at this later point. He explains that the event took place in stages: part occurred on the day that Bnei Yisrael first arrived in Eretz Yisrael, and part happened after the battles of Yericho and Ay.

39. *Mishbetzos Zahav* (p. 162) cites a similar idea from *sefer Lev Aharon*. He notes that, whereas in their initial conquests (i.e., against Yericho and Ay) the Jews razed the enemy cities, in the campaigns that followed they *settled* the conquered towns. The *Navi* records the episode of *Har Gerizim* and *Har Eival* at this point to signify that the Jews fully committed themselves to the Torah and its values and were ready to embark on the heart of their conquest and settlement of Eretz Yisrael.

קדוש, וכל אחד ואחד מישראל הוא איבר בשיעור קומת כנסת ישראל שהיא שכינתו יתברך...
עיקר טעמי ופנימיות המצוות לא שייך אלא בציבור.

[v] כלליות כנסת ישראל אין מובנה קבוץ כל הפרטים של האישים היחידים מבני ישראל.
אלא שהענין הוא להפך, דכלליות כנסת ישראל היא יחידה אחת אשר האישים היחידים הם
חלקים ממנה.

[vi] כשם שגאולת מצרים יצרה תורת צבור ישראל, כמו כן, קרבן פסח מחדש שם צבור על
הכנופיא אשר הוא בא בה.

[vii] ידוע גודל כח השפעת הצבור על היחיד שבתוכו. והעיד הכתוב שאילו היתה מעילה-
בחרם אצלם בריחוק ובביזוי ובתיעוב היותר אפשרי כראוי להם לפי מדרגתם בדביקות, לא
היה אפשר שימצא אפילו אחד שיעיז לגנוב.

[viii] בלי ספק, שאילו לא מעלו בחרם, היו נוצחים כל הארץ בלי עמל ובלי יגיעה בהשגחה
אלקית כעין יריחו, אלא ממה שנעעדרו על ידי עכן הוצרכו להלחם כדרך כל הארץ ועשו
מארב. ולכך הותר הותר שלל העי וכו', שכיון שאתם עושים תחבולה אנושית, ראוי שתבוזו לכם,
כי יגיע כפכם הוא.

Expanding
Their Focus

A FTER FOCUSING INITIALLY ON infusing their own lives and endeavors with holiness, Bnei Yisrael began to spread their influence and God's message throughout Eretz Yisrael to all its inhabitants.[1]

Inspire or Enforce

THE TORAH PROVIDES two contrasting visions of how that message might be spread:

A) The Torah's ideal envisions all nations recognizing Hashem's eminence and accepting the basic tenets of the Torah. The

---

1. This task required immense insight and aptitude. Some commentators write (see *Sha'arei Aharon, Devarim* 3:21) that it is for this reason that the Torah writes Yehoshua's name with an extra letter (*vav*) when he is first assigned this mission (*Devarim* ibid.). (Yehoshua's name is spelled this way in one other place in *Tanach* — *Sefer Shoftim* 2:7. It is possible that since the *pasuk* in *Shoftim* recaps Yehoshua's success, the *Navi* honored his achievements by spelling his name with an extra *vav* in that instance as well.)

Torah commands Bnei Yisrael to entreat its enemies to peacefully accept Hashem's sovereignty and to thus side-step the need for war.[2]

To be sure, the Torah does not instruct the Jewish people to forcibly convert non-Jews to Judaism. Members of other nations can accept Hashem's dominion on various levels. The most basic level is to agree to live as an upstanding human being — to accept the "seven *mitzvos Bnei Noach*," the most fundamental proprieties and tenets of the human race.[3] A non-Jew may wish to adopt an additional degree of holiness and become a "*ger toshav*," with

---

2. The *Rishonim* disagree as to whether Bnei Yisrael were permitted to accept peace treaties only *before* they entered Eretz Yisrael, or if they could trust their adversaries to make peace even *after* they entered Eretz Yisrael and began their conquest. Some commentators write that an enemy may be trusted if it is clear that the enemy is sincere. Others add that Bnei Yisrael may trust nations that propose peace of their own accord. For details, see *Nachalas Shimon* (7:3, 6; 35:1–4; ch. 35 addition #1).

3. See *Rambam* (*Hilchos Melachim* 9:1) for a listing of these *mitzvos*. (For further elaboration on their unique significance, see *Rambam, Hilchos Melachim* 8:11; see also my comments in *Toras HaKavod* 30:2.)

Rishonim seemingly disagree as to whether non-Jews who desire to remain in Eretz Yisrael need to accept *all* seven *mitzvos Bnei Noach*, or if it is sufficient that they assent to refrain from serving false deities. (See *Rambam, Hilchos Melachim* 6:1 and 8:10; *Sefer HaChinuch* #94, Mechon Yerushalayim ed., fn. 2; *Gur Aryeh, Shemos* 23:12, Mechon Yerushalayim ed., fn. 35.)

Of note, some *Rishonim* imply that it is not sufficient for a non-Jew who wishes to live in Eretz Yisrael to simply abide by the seven *mitzvos Bnei Noach*. To assure wholehearted acceptance of these *mitzvos*, the non-Jew may need to accept formal "*ger toshav*" status (see *Rambam, Hilchos Avodah Zarah* 10:6; *Raavad* and *Kesef Mishneh* ad loc.; *Chazon Ish, Yoreh De'ah* 65:3). The Rambam (ibid. 6:1) further maintains that non-Jewish inhabitants of Eretz Yisrael must accept Bnei Yisrael's full authority and pay taxes to them. But the Chazon Ish (*Chazon Ish, Even HaEzer* 146:4 s.v. ובסוף and s.v. לדעת) notes that others seem to disagree with this condition. He adds that even the Rambam would concede that people who accept the seven *mitzvos Bnei Noach* of their own accord may continue to live in peace without accepting Bnei Yisrael's political sovereignty.

its added benefits and obligations.[4] Another level yet of holiness can be attained by becoming a non-Jewish servant (*eved Canaani*), whereby the non-Jew gains the status of a "semi-Jew" and is obligated to adhere to most *mitzvos* of the Torah.[5] Finally, a non-Jew may become a full-fledged convert, enjoying complete status as a Jew.[6]

B) Should, however, the neighboring non-Jews decline to renounce *avodah zarah* and fail to uphold the seven *mitzvos Bnei Noach*,[7] the Torah sentences them to annihilation at

---

4. For some benefits of this status, see *Rambam* (*Hilchos Zechiyah U'Matanah* 3:11). For a good overview of the various opinions regarding the exact parameters of a *ger toshav*'s status and obligations, see *Encyclopedia Talmudit* (vol. 6, s.v. "*Ger Toshav*").

5. A non-Jewish servant enjoys a unique legal status somewhere between that of a Jew and a non-Jew. *Gemara Sanhedrin* (58b; *Chiddushei HaRan* ad loc.) describes that even though an *eved Canaani* is no longer a non-Jew, he nevertheless does not possess the complete holiness of a Jew — "יצא מכלל כותי, ולכלל ישראל לא בא". R. Yosef Engel (*Beis HaOtzar*, vol. 2, p. 10a) develops this idea further. Note also the phraseology of the Rambam (*Hilchos Issurei Bi'ah* 13:11–12). *Kovetz Yesodos VaChakiros* (s.v. עבד כנעני במצוות) points to various areas in halachah where a servant has a status similar to that of a Jew and others where he has a status similar to that of a non-Jew.

6. Members of some nationalities, however, may not be afforded the opportunity to convert. See *Nachalas Shimon* (*Shmuel II*, ch. 2 and 14:8) regarding accepting converts from the nations of Amalek, Amon, and Moav. Furthermore, not all converts enjoy equal status. Those who come from Amon, Moav, and Egypt (and possibly all of the Seven Nations; see *Nachalas Shimon*, ch. 25) are not afforded full rights as Jews (at least for a period of time) due to the evil dispositions that their ancestors introduced into their spiritual makeup. In truth, even regular converts, as exalted as they are due to their heroic choice to undergo such a laudable transformation, may retain some traits that they inculcated before becoming Jewish and remain somewhat distinct from those who were born Jewish. (See details in my essay published in the back of *The Daf B'Iyun: Berachos Perek 1* — "האם ראוי להינשא לגיורת" and in *Toras HaKavod*, ch. 28.)

7. According to some *Rishonim*, renouncing *avodah zarah*, even without accepting the seven *mitzvos Bnei Noach*, may be sufficient. See footnote 3 above.

the hands of the conquering Bnei Yisrael. Without at least the barest of moral standards, and without rudimentary recognition of the true Creator, these inhabitants would prove a menace to the Jewish people and to the world.[8]

The Torah views this latter scenario as far from ideal, and it warns against allowing a "holy crusade" to nurture cruelty, or even insensitivity, within the individual characters of the Jewish people.[9]

Flight, Truce, and Defiance

CHAZAL RECORD (*Yerushalmi Shevi'is* 6:1) that when Bnei Yisrael first approached Eretz Yisrael, they offered the aforementioned options to the local inhabitants along with the option of simply

---

8. It should be noted, however, that according to many *Rishonim*, this strict sentence applies only to the Seven Nations and to Amalek. These nations are so tenaciously attached to their evil ways and distorted values that they need to be destroyed. (*Rishonim* further debate whether the Seven Nations need to be destroyed even if they live outside of Eretz Yisrael.) For further details, see *Lechem Mishneh* (on *Rambam, Hilchos Melachim* 6:1); *Mitzvas HaMelech* (on Rambam's *Sefer HaMitzvos*, negative commandments 49–48#); *Nachalas Shimon* (35:6). There is also special significance ascribed to the lands adjacent to Eretz Yisrael (see *Mishbetzos Zahav*, pp. 213–4).

9. See, for example, the famous *pasuk* (*Mishlei* 24:17 — "בנפול אויבך אל תשמח") that proscribes rejoicing over the demise of one's enemy. *Chazal* also teach that joy must be curtailed during moments of an adversary's suffering, as such destruction is not considered "good" and God is not "pleased" with such events (see *Megillah* 10b; *Sanhedrin* 39b). The Chazon Ish (*Chazon Ish, Orach Chaim* 56:4 s.v. וכמ") explains that when punishing evildoers, we are commanded to feel deep pain and eschew intent for personal gain. The *Ohr HaChaim HaKadosh* (*Devarim* 13:18) adds that the Torah promises that if we follow its directives, Hashem will not allow our righteous brutality to dull our senses of mercy or concern for our fellow man. (For a lengthier discussion of this topic, see my essays, published in the back of *The Daf B'Iyun: Berachos Perek* 1 — "שמחה ותפילה על מפלתן של רשעים" and in *Toras HaKavod*, ch. 13.)

running away. The nations responded in various manners, but most chose to fight Bnei Yisrael: "The *Girgashi* nation believed in Hashem and fled to Africa; the *Givonim* made peace [with the Jews]; and thirty-one kings waged war and fell."[i]

Indeed, immediately after the conquests of Yericho and Ay and following the *Navi's* report of Bnei Yisrael's reaffirmation of the Torah at *Har Gerizim* and *Har Eival* — events that solidified the mission of the Jewish people (see the preceding chapter of this work) — the *Navi* records that "all the kings" banded together to fight against the Jews (9:1–2).[10] This alliance was not simply about territory and autonomy; it was about the supremacy of God. The moment these kings sensed that Bnei Yisrael intended to spread the word of God among their citizens and within their societies, they rallied instantly to thwart that effort. The nations inhabiting Eretz Yisrael had the opportunity to live in peace and harmony, but they did not wish to do so. Such peace would have entailed accepting Hashem's sovereignty, something they were utterly unwilling to concede.

The nations' response, as stated clearly in the *pasuk* (9:2), was (almost) unanimous ("פה אחד"). *Chazal* (*Yalkut Shimoni* #18)[ii] see this defiant response as echoing another incident in history when

---

10. *Girgashi* is conspicuously missing from this list of nations who joined together to fight, supporting *Chazal's* assertion above. *Girgashi* is likewise not mentioned in *Shemos* (33:2) among the nations that Bnei Yisrael will destroy. *Rashi* (ad loc.) notes this point and cites *Vayikra Rabbah* (17:6) that reports that the *Girgashim* fled Eretz Yisrael and were thus not destroyed, as described. Yet, *Girgashi* is mentioned later in *Sefer Yehoshua* (24:11) as one of the nations that fought Bnei Yisrael. *Mishbetzos Zahav* (24:11) explains that although most of *Girgashi* fled, some of them remained in Eretz Yisrael and waged war. *Yefeh To'ar* (*Vayikra Rabbah* ibid.) explains similarly. *Mishbetzos Zahav* (ibid.) further cites the Gra (*Aderes Eliyahu, Devarim* 20:17) who adds that the Torah (*Devarim* ibid.) alludes to *Girgashi* (see *Rashi* ad loc.) because some individual *Girgashim* remained in the land, but they are not listed *explicitly* because most of their nation fled.

the nations of the world united to battle Hashem — the construction of the Tower of Bavel (*Bereishis* 11:1–9; see *Rashi* ad loc. 11:1). Moreover, *Chazal* write, the response of these enemy kings also harbingers a future time when the nations will once again unite for this nefarious purpose and wage the war of *Gog U'Magog*.

The Givonim's Trap

ONLY THE PEOPLE of Givon appreciated that fighting would spell their doom. They therefore felt that they had no choice but to plead for peace with the Jews (9:3–6).

This affair with the *Givonim*, however, was not a simple one for Bnei Yisrael. The *Givonim* were not motivated by pure intentions. As *Chazal* write (*Bamidbar Rabbah* 8:4),[iii] the *Givonim*'s peace proposal was nothing more than a ploy designed to trip Bnei Yisrael — to cause them to sin and thereby sabotage their relationship with Hashem.[11] The *Givonim* wished to persuade Bnei Yisrael to spare them and to leave them within the borders of the Promised Land. Hashem, by the *Givonim*'s calculation, would then punish Bnei Yisrael for permitting one of the Seven Nations (which included the *Givonim*[12]) to remain in Eretz Yisrael.[13]

---

11. *Chazal* and various commentators (see *Mishbetzos Zahav* 9:7) draw parallels between the *Givonim* and the serpent that infamously tricked Chava into eating from the Tree of Knowledge (*Bereishis*, ch. 3). They further note that the *Givonim* were descendants of Shechem, who surreptitiously violated Yaakov's daughter, Dinah (*Bereishis* 34:1–2), in an attempt to contaminate the Jewish nation.

12. The *pesukim* seem to state clearly that the *Givonim* were part of the *Chivi* nation (see 9:7; 11:19; see also *Rashi* 9:4). But *Chazal* (*Bamidbar Rabbah* 8:4) explain that they really belonged to the *Emori*. (For more on the exact listing of the Seven Nations, see *Rashi* and other commentaries, *Devarim* 18:2.)

13. The text of the *Navi* itself implies that the *Givonim*'s intentions were not pure. As noted above (footnote 2), a number of commentators write that Bnei Yisrael

Hence, the Jews' treaty with Givon (9:15) represented a slight *deviation* from their mission, not a fulfillment of it.[14] The *Navi* indicates that the *Givonim* succeeded in deceiving the Jewish leadership only because the latter failed to seek counsel from Hashem (9:14).[15]

As the peace was negotiated under false pretenses, many members of Bnei Yisrael favored abrogating the treaty (9:18). Yet, Bnei Yisrael honored the treaty for fear of the possible desecration of Hashem's name (*chillul HaShem*) that could have resulted had they reneged (see *Gittin* 46a; *Nachalas Shimon*, ch. 35, fn. 7). They were forced to concede their mistake and make the best of a suboptimal situation.

Yehoshua, however, not only upheld the treaty; he surprisingly even hired the *Givonim* for key positions in the holy Mishkan (9:23)!

---

were permitted to accept peace arrangements in instances where the peace proposition was genuine. Had the *Givonim* intended to embrace Bnei Yisrael sincerely, they would not have needed to scheme as they did; rather, they would have simply approached Bnei Yisrael straightforwardly. (Some *Rishonim*, however, understand that the *Givonim* did not know that Bnei Yisrael were permitted to accept a peace proposal; see *Nachalas Shimon* 35:4.)

14. *Chazal* teach that Yehoshua was ultimately punished for this mistake. The punishment was meted out to his descendant, Yirmeyahu HaNavi, who suffered as a consequence of the Givon treaty (see *Kallah Rabbasi*, end of ch. 4; see also *The Navi Journey*, pp. 112–3 for further explication).

15. Commentators add (see *Rashi* and *Mishbetzos Zahav* 9:4) that Bnei Yisrael succumbed to the *Givonim's* trickery as Divine retribution for the deception that Bnei Yisrael's ancestors perpetrated against the *Givonim's* ancestors (Yaakov's sons tricked the inhabitants of Shechem; see *Bereishis*, ch. 34).

Chazal (*Midrash Tanchuma, Netzavim* #2; *Yevamos* 79a) also contrast Bnei Yisrael's response in the present episode with their response to the *Givonim's* request for peace in Moshe's time. Unlike Yehoshua, Moshe wisely rejected the *Givonim's* disingenuous offer. (See, however, *Rashi, Devarim* 29:10, who seemingly understands that Moshe accepted the enemy's appeal. Yet, according to *Rashi*, it was the *Canaanim* who approached Moshe, not the *Givonim*. For further analysis of that story, see *Gur Aryeh* ad loc. along with other commentators.)

At first glance this decision seems rather bizarre. Although the logic proposed by many of Bnei Yisrael's leaders to keep the *Givonim* in check by utilizing them as servants (9:21) is quite sensible, Yehoshua's resolution (see *Ralbag* and *Radak* ad loc.) to appoint them as esteemed employees of the Mishkan begs explanation.[16] More troubling yet is *Chazal's* assertion that Yehoshua converted the *Givonim* to Judaism (see *Nachalas Shimon*, ch. 35, addition #1, s.v. והנה)![17] Why would he accept these charlatans as converts?!

In fact, Yehoshua's approach was brilliant. He recognized that, for better or worse, the *Givonim* were there to stay. To mitigate their negative moral and spiritual influence on Bnei Yisrael, the best option was to integrate them, at least to a degree, so that they would learn better values and align their standards with those of Bnei Yisrael. Yehoshua therefore converted them and employed them in an insulated, spiritually rich environment, with the hope that these efforts would, in time, help the *Givonim* absorb and reflect the Torah's ideals.[18] At the same time, however, Yehoshua took necessary precautions and forbade the *Givonim* from marrying freely within the Jewish nation (see *Radak* 9:21; *Nachalas Shimon, Shmuel II*, ch. 39), lest they lead members of Bnei Yisrael astray.[19]

---

16. Commentators are indeed quite bothered by this question; see *Nachalas Shimon* (35:12 s.v. שו"ר and fn. 7).

17. Some commentators argue, however, that not *all* members of Givon converted (see *Nachalas Shimon, Shmuel II*, vol. 2, 39:5).

18. R. Gershon Weiss *shlita* is quoted as offering a similar understanding of Yehoshua's decision (see *The Navi Journey*, p. 115).

19. Unfortunately, however, the *Givonim* did not integrate Torah values, as is clear from *Shmuel II* (21:2–6; see also *Bamidbar Rabbah* 8:4). Later generations of Jews had to continue ostracizing them (see *Nachalas Shimon* ibid.).

Bnei Yisrael's Success

AS MENTIONED, ASIDE from the *Givonim* and *Girgashim*, the rest of the inhabitants of Eretz Yisrael waged war against Hashem and the Jewish nation. The *Navi* informs us (11:19–20) that Hashem ensured that most of the nations would opt to fight, as He did not want these nations to remain in Eretz Yisrael and corrupt the Jews spiritually. He knew that, no matter what pledges these nations might make when negotiating peace, they would eventually revert to their old idolatrous ways and inflict both physical and spiritual harm on the Jewish people (see *Radak* 11:20; see also *Bamidbar* 33:55).

As Bnei Yisrael battled their enemies, they tried not only to win wars but to concomitantly proclaim Hashem's greatness. After all, spreading piety and virtue was their primary objective. In line with this mission, Yehoshua asked Hashem to miraculously halt the path of the sun and suspend it in the sky, so that the entire world would witness His greatness (10:12–14; see *Nachalas Shimon* 36:3).[20] [Some add that Yehoshua wanted to make clear that Hashem protects Bnei Yisrael's allies — the *Givonim*. Yehoshua therefore requested that specifically the war fought to defend the *Givonim* be exceedingly miraculous; see *Mishbetzos Zahav* (p. 192).] Yehoshua further displayed the Jews' dominance over evil by placing his officers' feet mockingly on the necks of the enemy kings

---

20. Some commentators, however, understand that the sun paused only over that particular battlefield but not throughout the world (see *Nachalas Shimon* ibid.). (R. Dessler, in *Michtav Me'Eliyahu*, vol. 1, p. 308, develops, with his unique profundity, how such a phenomenon could exist.) The Ralbag offers an additional, novel interpretation that the sun did not actually stop at all. Rather, he explains, Hashem brought about Bnei Yisrael's victory very quickly, *as if* time had stopped. (For explanation as to why some *Rishonim* choose to explain various ostensible miracles in *Tanach* in more natural terms, see *Emes L'Yaakov*, *Avos* 5:5, fn. 132; see also *Michtav Me'Eliyahu*, vol. 4 pp. 354–5.)

(10:24; see also *Devarim* 33:29).[21] Likewise, Bnei Yisrael crippled enemy horses and burned their chariots to demonstrate that trust must be placed in the Almighty, not in physical war machines (see 11:6 with *Malbim*).[22]

But, while Yehoshua and the army at his command made impressive strides at awakening the inhabitants in and around Eretz Yisrael to the presence and providence of God, they fell far short of finishing the job (see *Rashi* 11:18, along with our comments, end of *Perakim* 13–21). That assignment remained with Bnei Yisrael throughout Yehoshua's reign and would continue to drive the Jewish nation throughout history.[23]

---

21. Similar tactics were used by other great leaders in *Tanach* (see *Sefer Shoftim* 1:6 with *Ralbag*; see also *Shmuel II* 12:31). It should be noted that, throughout history, generals from secular and/or evil nations degraded defeated armies with symbolic gestures similar to those employed by the righteous men referred to above. The distinction between these episodes, however, is readily apparent. As noted earlier (footnote 9), the righteous carry out these acts truly for God. They are pained by the need to cause others to suffer and by the necessity to act in an ostensibly cruel manner. They also try to uphold the basic dignity afforded all people, who, by virtue of being human, reflect the "image of God." Indeed, Yehoshua, due to this very sentiment, did not allow the bodies of his enemies to remain on public display for very long, and he afforded them a makeshift burial (10:26–27; see *Nachalas Shimon*, ch. 29). Secular generals, on the other hand, often perform such acts for self-aggrandizement, care little about their enemy's plight, and do not expend any effort to uphold the victim's human dignity. The fact that the two scenarios — the one carried out by the righteous and the one performed by the secular or evil — appear similar is nothing more than a distorted illusion. It is a prime example of Shlomo HaMelech's dictum that "זה לעומת זה עשה האלקים" (*Koheles* 7:14) — Hashem created every "positive" entity with its "negative" counterpart. (For more examples of this concept, see, among numerous other sources, R. Tzaddok HaKohen, *Takkanas HaShavin*, 13b s.v. וידוע; 22b s.v. וכל; 23b s.v. ואלו.)

22. Regarding the halachic concerns involved in paining animals and unnecessarily destroying usable objects, see *Nachalas Shimon* (ch. 37).

23. In truth, Bnei Yisrael's ultimate goal is to spread Godliness not only throughout Eretz Yisrael but throughout the entire *world*. Tradition indicates (see *Yalkut Shimoni, Yeshayah* #503; *Bris Moshe* on *Smag*, negative commandments 276:2) that

ENDNOTES

[i] אמר ר' שמואל, ג' פרסטיניות (פי' צווי המלך בכתב) שלח יהושע לארץ ישראל עד שלא יכנסו לארץ. מי שהוא רוצה להפנות יפנה, להשלים ישלים, לעשות מלחמה יעשה. גרגשי פינה והאמין לו להקב"ה והלך לו לאפריקי וכו', גבעונים השלימו... שלשים ואחד מלך עשו מלחמה ונפלו.

[ii] א"ר אייבו בשם ר"א בנו של ר"י הגלילי, בשלשה מקומות חלקו באי עולם על הקב"ה. א' בדור ההפלגה, 'ויהי כל הארץ שפה אחת', ומהו 'ודברים אחדים', דברים של חירופין... וא' בימי גוג ומגוג, 'יתיצבו מלכי ארץ, ורוזנים נוסדו יחד על ה' ועל משיחו'. וא' בימי יהושע, שנאמר 'ויתקבצו יחדיו להלחם עם יהושע ועם ישראל פה אחד', מהו 'פה אחד', שחלקו על הקב"ה שנא' בו 'שמע ישראל ה' אלקינו ה' אחד'.

[iii] [הגבעונים] מן האמרי היו. ולמה קורא אותן 'חוי' (יהושע ט:ז), על שעשו מעשה חוי – מעשה נחש... כך עשו הגבעונים: אמרו, יודעים אנו שאמר הקב"ה לישראל 'כי החרם תחרימם, החתי והאמרי וגו'" (דברים כ:יז), 'לא תכרת להם ברית וגו'" (דברים ז:ב). אלא הרי אנו הולכין ומרמין בהם והם כורתים אתנו ברית. מה נפשך, יהרגו אותנו – יעברו על השבועה. יקיימו אותנו – עוברים על הגזרה. בין כך ובין כך נענשים, ואנו יורשין את הארץ לעצמנו.

in the End of Days, by spreading holiness of sufficient degree, Bnei Yisrael will confer the status of Eretz Yisrael on the entire world. (Some add that this holiness will spread from Eretz Yisrael to the rest of the world by means of the lands of *Ever HaYarden*; see *Kosleinu, Kovetz Yeshivat HaKotel*, vol. 14, pp. 279–80 fn. 59.)

PERAKIM 13–21:

Settling and
Sanctifying the Land

AFTER CRYSTALLIZING THEIR NATIONAL unity and purpose, and after conquering much of the land and spreading God's message, Bnei Yisrael were finally ready to
allocate the territory and settle down in their new home.

The apportionment of Eretz Yisrael was not simply a division
of property. Rather, it represented the next stage of imbuing the
land with eternal sanctity.[1]

---

1. Hashem instructed Yehoshua to apportion the land even though Bnei Yisrael
had not completed their conquest (see 13:1–7). It can be explained that Hashem
wished for Yehoshua specifically, as opposed to a subsequent leader, to lead this
process with his supreme holiness and purity. Additionally, it seems that after
years of fighting, the war-weary people were anxious to return to their own families and tribes (life during wartime was exceedingly difficult, as recorded in *Midrash Tanchuma, Metzora* #6). Yehoshua appreciated that some battles — and
some territory — would have to wait for another generation and another leader.
Those battles, though, would be fought not by a united national Jewish army but
by individual tribes or groups of tribes (as described in *Sefer Shoftim, Perek* 1). In
order to confer the formal spiritual status of "Eretz Yisrael" upon the entire territory, such that all parts of the land would forever retain that irrevocable stature,
Yehoshua and his court, representing the nation as a complete whole, formally
divided the entire country — even the parts that had yet to be conquered (see
Rambam, Hilchos Terumos 1:2).

On a halachic level, Bnei Yisrael were not obligated in the laws of *terumah, ma'aser,* or *shemittah* until they conquered and settled the land (see *Sifra, Behar* 25:2; *Tosefta, Makkos* 2:1). That is, the fruit of Eretz Yisrael did not fully reflect the land's holiness until Bnei Yisrael triggered that latent sanctity by formally establishing the land as their home. (And indeed, when some of the tribes of Bnei Yisrael were later expelled from the Land, Eretz Yisrael lost some of its holiness, and the laws of *Yovel* expired; see *Rambam, Hilchos Shemittah V'Yovel* 10:8.)

Due to the significance of this enterprise, it is understandable that the exact order in which Bnei Yisrael settled the Land, and the *Navi*'s recording of it, was not happenstance, but precise and full of meaning.

Moshe's Role in Settling Eretz Yisrael

THE *NAVI* REVIEWS Moshe's conquest of *Ever HaYarden* before listing the lands that Yehoshua conquered (see 12:1–6). Likewise, the *Navi* opens the chapter of apportioning Eretz Yisrael with an inventory of the settlements established by Reuven, Gad, and half of Menashe in *Ever HaYarden* (13:8-32). Why is it important for the *Navi* to catalogue Moshe's conquests and his division of *Ever HaYarden*?

The *Navi* seemingly aims to highlight that Yehoshua, when conquering and dividing Eretz Yisrael, built upon the foundation established by his mentor, Moshe Rabbeinu. The Abarbanel (14:1) writes: "Just as Moshe, by himself, apportioned the land that is across (east of) the Yarden — *in that very same fashion,* Elazar, Yehoshua, and the heads of the families inherited and divided the entire land [of Israel] among the nine-and-a-half tribes."[i] Yehoshua wished to tap into the sanctity that Moshe instilled in this endeavor.

Indeed, it was extremely important to Moshe Rabbeinu to

play a part in the conquest of Eretz Yisrael. The *pesukim* (*Devarim* 3:23–25) recount Moshe's relentless prayers to the Almighty to allow him to see and enter Eretz Yisrael with his people. *Chazal* (*Devarim Rabbah* 11:10) elaborate further, describing Moshe's piercing cries and his astounding 515 prayers regarding this issue. And indeed, Hashem granted Moshe a portion of his wish (see *Rashi, Devarim* 3:27; *Sifrei, Pinchas* #135): although Moshe was not permitted to physically enter Eretz Yisrael, he was nevertheless allowed to view it from atop *Har Nevo* (located in trans-Jordan).[2]

How, though, was Hashem's concession that Moshe see Eretz Yisrael considered even a *partial* fulfillment of Moshe's true request? How did it help for Moshe to view the land from afar?[3] Rav Ahron Lopiansky *shlita* explains that Moshe's glance at Eretz Yisrael paved the way for Bnei Yisrael's success in their conquest.[4] Moshe embodied the "eyes" of Bnei Yisrael. He provided the nation with an eternal vision and with a lasting connection to the land. Furthermore, commentators explain that Moshe's visual scan of

---

2. Moshe's ascension of a mountain to see Eretz Yisrael is mentioned a number of times in the Torah (*Bamidbar* 27:12; *Devarim* 3:27; 32:49; 34:1). Commentators write that all instances refer to the same mountain and to the same event (see *Sha'arei Aharon, Pinchas* 27:12).

3. Doubly surprising, the Maharal (*Gur Aryeh, Devarim* 3:27) seemingly maintains that seeing Eretz Yisrael (as opposed to entering it) constituted Moshe's *foremost* request. (R. Yehoshua Hartman *shlita* (*Gur Aryeh* ibid., fn. 75) expresses bewilderment over this point.) In a similar vein, *Chazal* (*Sifrei* ibid.) further stress that Moshe viewed Eretz Yisrael in its *entirety*; he was shown "unrevealed parts" of the land and sections that even Yehoshua did not merit to traverse. The *Ohr HaChaim HaKadosh* (*Bamidbar* 27:13) explains that Hashem showed Moshe hidden, spiritual aspects of the land that can be seen only through the special *Ohr HaGanuz* (Concealed Light).

4. We have already mentioned (*Perakim 1–4*; see also *Mishbetzos Zahav* pp. 3, 330) that had Moshe Rabbeinu *physically* led Bnei Yisrael into Eretz Yisrael, the conquest would have been infused with such intense holiness that the Beis HaMikdash would have been built promptly and never destroyed.

Eretz Yisrael imparted spiritual energy (which can occur through the gaze of righteous people) that assisted Bnei Yisrael in their campaigns (see *Tzror HaMor, Bamidbar* 34:2, *Devarim* 32:48–9; *Sha'arei Aharon, Devarim* 3:27).[5]

The Netziv (*Ha'Amek Davar, Devarim* 3:28) similarly links Moshe's panoramic survey of the land with Bnei Yisrael's later success:[ii]

> Through this, that you (Moshe) will see [Eretz Yisrael], Yehoshua's heart will feel assured that he will certainly conquer [Eretz Yisrael]. For this is a general rule regarding the promise of a prophet: when [a prophecy] leaves the [theoretical] realm of [Divine] "decree" and [enters the realm of physical reality] through some miniscule action [that is] similar to it (the prophecy), that [action] serves as a sign that it (the prophecy) will certainly occur[6]... Therefore, Hashem began to show Moshe the land, so that it would [undoubtedly] be conquered by Yehoshua and Yisrael.

In truth, Moshe supplied more than just the vision for Bnei Yisrael's conquest; he actually began the process of conquering and apportioning Eretz Yisrael. Moshe led Bnei Yisrael in the wars against Sichon and Og in *Ever HaYarden*, and he assigned the conquered territory to the two-and-a-half tribes. Controlling these lands represented Bnei Yisrael's first strides toward founding their

---

5. The *Tzror HaMor* adds that by mentioning that Moshe ascended the mountain "opposite Yericho," the *pasuk* (*Devarim* 32:49) alludes to the fact that the Jewish people would enter and conquer Eretz Yisrael (beginning with the battle of Yericho) in Moshe's merit.

6. The Netziv notes that the Ramban (*Bereishis* 12:6) refers to this concept as well. (To explain this idea on a basic level: humans relate to things that are physical. For example, offering a *gift* to a loved one often has a more lasting impact than simply *professing* one's love. Similarly, *mitzvos* must be performed physically, not just thought about and considered. Hence, when a decree or prophecy is accompanied by a concrete action, it takes root in our material world and has a lasting effect.)

homeland.[7] This territory, although not part of Eretz Yisrael proper, enjoys a partial-Eretz Yisrael status (see *Mishbetzos Zahav* 12:6, 22:5, 22:19; *Nachalas Shimon*, ch. 54). Furthermore, these lands were included in Hashem's promise to Avraham Avinu, and, in the End of Days, they, along with other adjacent lands on the eastern side of the Yarden, will belong to Bnei Yisrael (see *Bereishis Rabbah* 44:23; *Rashi, Devarim* 18:2). There are even some indications in *Chazal* and various commentators that, in the time of Mashiach, *Ever HaYarden* will attain *full status* of Eretz Yisrael (see R. Zev Hoberman *zt"l's Lechem Chuki*, ch. 17–18). So symbolically significant were the victories over Sichon and Og that Moshe presumed, after experiencing Divine help in these battles, that Hashem had voided the decree preventing him from leading the Jews into Eretz Yisrael proper (see *Rashi, Devarim* 3:23 s.v. בעת, 3:24 s.v. אשר).[8]

Hence, when Yehoshua was called upon to conquer and apportion Eretz Yisrael, he was not *beginning* a process, but *finishing* the work that Moshe had already begun! The *Navi* reminds us of this fact by reviewing Moshe's accomplishments in *Ever HaYarden* before relating Yehoshua's contribution.

---

7. The Ramban (*Bamidbar* 31:23) writes that some *halachos* governing the conquest of Eretz Yisrael (such as permission to eat non-kosher food; see above, *Perakim* 5–8, fn. 27) applied to the conquest of Sichon and Og's territory. The *Ba'alei HaTosafos* (*Hadar Zekeinim, Bamidbar* ad loc.), however, disagree, maintaining that only Yehoshua's battles in Eretz Yisrael proper enjoyed the halachic status of *kibbush ha'aretz* (conquering the Land).

8. The fact that Moshe was most intimately connected to *Ever HaYarden* may also help explain why the tribes of Reuven and Gad desired to remain in that area. They wanted to settle in the part of Eretz Yisrael that the great Moshe Rabbeinu personally conquered and instilled with holiness. Indeed, a number of commentators write that the tribes of Reuven and Gad felt extreme closeness to Moshe and wished to remain near the place of his interment. (See *Rashi, Devarim* 33:21; R. David Weiss's *Megadim Chadashim, Bamidbar* 32:1, quoting the Chozeh of Lublin and others.) For another related approach, see *Beis Yishai* (*Derashos* #35, s.v. והנה כך).

The Allotment

YEHOSHUA BEGAN PARTITIONING Eretz Yisrael with the tribe of Yehudah (14:6–15:63) and the remaining tribes of Yosef — Ephraim and the half of Menashe that had not settled in *Ever HaYarden* (16:1–17:18). Yehudah and Yosef received their portions first because they are leaders of Bnei Yisrael (*Radak* 12:23; *Malbim* 18:2; *Aderes Eliyahu* 15:1) and because their territory established Eretz Yisrael's borders — Yehudah in the South and Yosef in the North (*Radak* and *Aderes Eliyahu* 15:1).[9] Their portions provided the framework within which the other tribes would receive their shares.[10]

Before apportioning the remainder of the land, Yehoshua added yet another monumental element to the holiness of the nascent Jewish settlement — *Mishkan Shiloh*. *Mishbetzos Zahav* (bottom of p. 267, based on *Rashi, Bava Metzia* 89a s.v. נתחייבו) notes that the full holiness of Eretz Yisrael's agricultural produce

---

9. The *Navi* states (see 18:5) that Yosef's portion is in the North. *Radak* (18:5) seems to understand the *pasuk* as localizing Yosef's portion to the northern border of Eretz Yisrael. But Rashi explains the *pasuk* as saying that the tribes of Yosef received the most northern land *of that which was conquered thus far*. The explanation of the *Radak* seems rather difficult, for it is clear from simply glancing at a map that there are a number of tribes situated north of Yosef's portion! (*Divrei Tovah, Yehoshua*, vol. 3, 16:1 p. 731, makes a similar point.) Perhaps the *Radak* means simply that the tribes of Yosef were situated in the northern region of Eretz Yisrael. Therefore, through Yehudah and Yosef, Bnei Yisrael had strongholds on all sides, even though the territory of the tribes of Yosef did not actually reach the border. (*Oznayim LaTorah, Pinchas*, bottom of pp. 310–311, similarly explains that Yehudah could protect the south, Yosef the north, and the two-and-a-half *Shevatim* the east.)

10. The *Radak* (12:23) notes, however, that settling the border cities, paradoxically, led Bnei Yisrael to grow somewhat lax with respect to their unfinished military campaign. Once Yehudah and Yosef received their land, Bnei Yisrael felt that Eretz Yisrael was already under their control and that they did not need to be as vigilant in completing its conquest.

(along with the laws of tithing) was not actualized until *Mishkan Shiloh* was built.[11] The Mishkan of Shiloh was a more permanent structure than its predecessor (see *Zevachim* 112b; see *Rashi* and *Radak* 18:1), and it centralized communal worship.[12] Its dedication invited the Divine Presence that helped the remaining tribes expedite the completion of their conquest (see *Rashi* and *Metzudos David* 18:1).[13]

---

11. A number of sources indicate that the agricultural *mitzvos* took effect a bit later, after the remainder of the tribes settled their lands. Yet, since those settlements occurred soon after the establishment of *Mishkan Shiloh*, and since they depended upon Divine assistance provided in the wake of *Mishkan Shiloh*'s construction (see below), Rashi attributes commencement of these *mitzvos* to the building of *Mishkan Shiloh*. See *Hadras Kodesh* (R. Menashe Miller, *Yehoshua*, pp. 82–3); *Divrei Tovah* (R. Avraham Taub, *Yehoshua*, vol. 3, pp. 794–5).

12. During the era of *Mishkan Shiloh*, Bnei Yisrael were not permitted to serve Hashem on private altars (*bamos*); sacrificial worship was restricted to this singular location (see *Zevachim* ibid. and 119a). Many sources indicate (see *Mishbetzos Zahav*, p. 269) that similar to the eventual Beis HaMikdash in Yerushalayim, *Mishkan Shiloh* even carried an obligation of *aliyah la're'gel* (visiting the Temple, or, in this case, the *Mishkan*, during the holidays of Pesach, Shavuos, and Succos). (Regarding the contrast between *Mishkan Shiloh* and the Beis HaMikdash, see *Mishbetzos Zahav*, pp. 269–72; R. Zalman Sorotzkin's *Oznaim LaTorah*, *Devarim* 12:5, 9. With Hashem's help, I hope to further expound upon this topic in our notes on *Shmuel I*.)

13. *Divrei Tovah* (ibid., pp. 793–4) explains that the "division of the land," which lasted for an astounding seven years, included more than just surveying and assigning lots. Once the tribes were granted their lands, they continued to conquer those territories to enable their full settlement. (This point is also implied from the *pesukim*; see, for example, 18:2–3 with the commentary of *Metzudos David* ad loc.) Whereas the tribes of Yehudah and Yosef expended much time and effort conquering their portions of Eretz Yisrael, the tribes that received their allotments after the establishment of *Mishkan Shiloh* overtook their lands quickly and easily.

It should be further noted that while *Mishkan Shiloh* provided the Jewish people with the requisite sanctity to succeed in their remaining campaigns, the opposite is also true: the sanctity resulting from the Jewish people's conquests paved the way for the establishment of this holy Mishkan. *Mishbetzos Zahav* (p. 268) comments that *Mishkan Shiloh* could be erected only after much of Bnei

Yehoshua then divided the territory among the various tribes and added one final element of holiness to the land: the "cities of refuge" (*arei miklat*) and the "cities of *Levi'im*" (*perakim* 20–21).[14] These cities represented havens of holiness, populated by *Levi'im* and other saintly personalities.[15] In the *arei miklat*, wrongdoers who required self-reflection and atonement for their misdeeds could reside among the righteous in the hope of assimilating a healthier and more spiritual lifestyle (see *Sefer HaChinuch* #408; *Mishbetzos Zahav* pp. 283–4). The cities of *Levi'im* likewise served, to a great extent, as cities of refuge (where those guilty of accidental manslaughter could escape reprisal from a victim's next of kin; for details, see *Makkos* 10a and *Rambam, Hilchos Rotze'ach* 8:9–10). Together, the cities of refuge and cities of *Levi'im* provided Bnei Yisrael with the holiness of the tribe of Levi dispersed throughout Eretz Yisrael.

We mentioned previously (see our concluding notes to *Perakim* 9–12) that Yehoshua did not quite complete the task of

---

Yisrael already conquered and settled their lands, for the sanctity of *Mishkan Shiloh* rested upon the holiness established by the nation.

14. As we described above regarding the conquest and division of Eretz Yisrael, here too, Yehoshua was completing what Moshe had already started. Moshe *designated* some *arei miklat*, but it was Yehoshua who *actualized* their capabilities, as even those *arei miklat* designated by Moshe became functional only once Yehoshua conquered and settled the land (see the following footnote; *Gemara Makkos* 9b; *Rashi, Bamidbar* 35:13). The text alludes to the fact that Yehoshua was completing Moshe's initiative by introducing Hashem's charge to Yehoshua on this occasion with language usually reserved for Moshe (20:1 — "וידבר ה' אל יהושע לאמר"; see *Mishbetzos Zahav* ad loc.). Moreover, Hashem makes specific mention of Moshe in His command to Yehoshua (see 20:2).

15. The *Tosefta* (*Makkos* 2:1) teaches that the *arei miklat* (like the laws of *ma'asar* and *shemittah*, mentioned above) became operative only once all of Eretz Yisrael was "conquered and settled." Because these cities contained unique holiness, activation and actualization of their protective function was dependent upon Bnei Yisrael settling Eretz Yisrael, an act that conferred the requisite sanctity upon the land.

conquering — and thereby fully settling and sanctifying — all of Eretz Yisrael. The *Maharsha* (*Bava Basra* 122a)[iii] explains that Yehoshua's division of Eretz Yisrael was "of this world" — ephemeral, performed by man, and incomplete. The future allotment, however, will be conducted by Hashem Himself — it will last forever and provide each tribe with all its necessities. The future will see the designation of additional sacred "cities of refuge" (see *Tosefta Makkos* 2:3; *Rambam, Hilchos Rotze'ach* 8:4). Additionally, a number of commentators opine that although the tribe of Levi did not receive a full, contiguous portion of Eretz Yisrael during Yehoshua's reign (something the *Navi* stresses numerous times — 13:14; 13:33; 14:3; 18:7),[16] they will merit a full portion in future times (see *Rashbam, Bava Basra* 122a s.v. תניא ועוד).[17] Hence,

---

16. Commentators debate how to precisely characterize the portion of Eretz Yisrael that the *Levi'im* received. Were their cities truly considered an inheritance (נחלה), owned by the tribe of Levi? Or were they merely locales in which *Levi'im* had the right to live, but the real estate belonged to the tribe in whose territory each such city was located (see 21:2 — "ערים לשבת")? (See *Ma'aser Sheini* 5:14; *Tosafos* and *Tosafos HaRosh, Berachos* 20b s.v. נשים; R. Shlomo Wahrman *zt"l*'s *She'eris Yosef*, vol. 3 #48; *Abarbanel* 13:32–33. For a discussion as to whether there is a distinction, in this regard, between *Kohanim* and *Levi'im*, see *Nachalas Shimon* 52:5, with fn. 12 and addition #1.)

17. In a similar vein, some sources indicate that, in future times, converts too will receive land in Eretz Yisrael, even though they were excluded from the original apportionment (see *Nachalas Shimon*, ch. 38; *Lechem Chuki*, ch. 6).

The Gemara (*Bava Basra* ibid.) also states that Mashiach will receive a portion of the land. (But commentators dispute the meaning of this Talmudic remark; see *Rambam, Hilchos Melachim* 4:8; *Igros Moshe, Orach Chaim*, vol. 2, #113, s.v. ואגב).

It is also possible that Shimon, like Levi, will receive a better lot in the future. The Gra (*Bei'ur HaGra, Yehoshua* 19:1) writes that the curse Yaakov Avinu gave Shimon and Levi (see *Bereishis* 49:5–7) tainted those tribes' territorial allotments. Shimon's portion was completely circumscribed by Yehudah's territory, much as the Levite cities were surrounded by their host tribes (see *Nachalas Shimon*, ch. 47 with addition #1).

It should be noted, however, that some commentators question the notion that the halachah will change in future times (i.e., that the *Levi'im* [and possibly

although in the twilight of Yehoshua's day, Eretz Yisrael remained far from fully settled and far from its maximal spiritual potential, the future will see a full realization of Yehoshua's mission and dream.

ENDNOTES

[i] כמו שמשה לבדו חלק הארץ אשר מעבר הירדן, באותו הדרך בעצמו נחלו וחלקו אלעזר ויהושע וראשי האבות את הארץ כלה לתשעה השבטים וחצי.

[ii] בזה שתראה [ארץ ישראל], יתחזק לב יהושע שבודאי יגיע הוא לידי כבישה. דזה כלל בהבטחת הנביא, כאשר יוצא מכח הגזרה לאיזה פעולה קלה מעין הדבה, אות היא שתתקיים בלי ספק... משום הכי החל ה' להראות למשה את הארץ, שתהא נכבשת ליהושע וישראל.

[iii] חלוקת עולם הזה היה דבר שלא היה לו קיום נצחי. היה נחלק בגורל, גם לא היה לכל א' דבר שלם כל הצורך לו. וע"כ לא היה גם ללוים חלק בו, שהם נחלת ה'. אבל לעולם הבא שיהיה חלוקה נצחית, תהיה על פי ה', והוא יחלוק חלק גם לנחלתו הלוים, ויהיה לכל אחד כל צרכו.

---

others] will receive land in the future); see *Chiddushei HaRan; Kovetz Shiurim* (*Bava Basra* ibid.); see also *Rashi* (*Devarim* 18:2). For some justifications as to how the *halachos* governing Levi's territory may change, see *Einayim LaMishpat* (*Bava Basra* ibid.); *Bris Moshe* (on *Smag*, negative commandment #276:2); *Yemos HaMashiach B'Halachah* (vol. 1, ch. 36). (For more on the general question whether *mitzvos* can change in future times, see *Rashba, Peirushei HaHaggados, Berachos* 12b; *Abarbanel, Rosh Amanah*, ch. 13, *safek* #4, s.v. ואין להקשות אם יביא, s.v. ומה שהביא החכם, s.v. ואפשר עוד ללכת; *Kovetz Shiurim*, vol. 2, 29:1; *Otzros Acharis HaYamim*, ch. 12; R. Netanel Wiederblank, *Illuminating Jewish Thought — Explorations of Free Will, Afterlife, and the Messianic Era*, pp. 547–579.)

PERAKIM 22–24:

Yehoshua's Legacy

B EFORE PASSING ON, YEHOSHUA sought to ensure that his life's work would have a lasting effect — that Bnei Yisrael would continue to follow the path he paved for them.

Timeless Remarks and Lasting Impact

YEHOSHUA SUMMONED THE tribes of Reuven, Gad, and half of Menashe and adjured them to pledge that they would uphold the Torah even as they returned to their homes in *Ever HaYarden* (22:5). He reminded his people of the great feats that Hashem performed for them (23:3; 23:9–10; 23:14; 24:2–13). He encouraged them to finish the task of conquering Eretz Yisrael, and he assured them that Hashem would offer assistance as long as they remained faithful to Him (23:4–6; 23:11–13). Yehoshua also warned that Hashem would sorely punish them should they disobey Him (23:15–16). He concluded his charge by exhorting Bnei Yisrael to cling to Hashem and His Torah and by obliging them to back their promise to do so with an oath (24:14–25). He urged them to put this promise into practice and to abandon all thought of deviating from Hashem (24:23). Finally, he publicly recorded the Torah's laws as well as Bnei Yisrael's promise in hope that their pact would truly

105

last forever (24:26–27; *Targum* and *Metzudos David* ad loc.[1]). Bnei Yisrael emphatically accepted Yehoshua's charge (24:16–18; 24:21; 24:24).

Bnei Yisrael's resolve was further evident from their daring response to the two-and-a-half tribes, whom the majority of Jews (those who settled in Eretz Yisrael proper) viewed as rebelling against God and splintering the nation. This majority was remarkably and laudably willing to do whatever necessary to preserve religious observance and national unity. If force was required, they were prepared to fight; if persuasion would work, they were willing to cede portions of their own territory to their wayward brethren (22:11–12; 22:16–20; see *Mishbetzos Zahav* p. 320). In confronting the two-and-a-half tribes, Bnei Yisrael explicitly expressed (22:20) that they learned their lesson from the Achan fiasco (see our comments to *Perakim* 5–8). They demonstrated their appreciation of the precept that each individual Jew is responsible for the physical and spiritual wellbeing of his fellow Jew. And the two-and-a-half tribes, for their part, never meant to secede. They shared the same sentiments as their brethren and erected a monument in hopes of retaining that national integrity and unity (see 22:10; 22:24–29; 22:34).

The *Navi*[2] attests that Yehoshua did a marvelous job in guiding Bnei Yisrael through a crucial junction in history. The *Navi* awards Yehoshua, at the end of his life, the appellation *"eved Hashem"* ("servant of God" — 24:29), the same description written of Moshe Rabbeinu in the beginning of the *Sefer* (1:1). The text records (24:31) that Bnei Yisrael continued to follow Yehoshua's

---

1. It should be noted that the Gemara (*Makkos* 11a) and *Malbim* (24:26) explain this passage differently; see there.

2. The Gemara (*Bava Basra* 15a) records that although Yehoshua authored most of *Sefer Yehoshua*, the final *pesukim* were written by Elazar and Pinchas.

instruction well after his passing. *Chazal* add (*Tanna D'vei Eliyahu Rabbah*, ch. 17)[i] that Yehoshua inspired Bnei Yisrael to accept "the kingship of Heaven out of love [of Hashem]." As a consequence of this love, Hashem displayed extra affection toward His people for three hundred years, throughout the period of the *Shoftim*.[3] *Mishkan Shiloh*, built under Yehoshua's directive, also remained with the nation for hundreds of years, sustaining the spirituality that Yehoshua inspired.

To be sure, as described in the opening chapter of this work, Yehoshua's "light" was distinct from that of Moshe. *Chazal* (*Bava Basra* 75a) compare Moshe to the sun and Yehoshua to the moon. Moshe possessed the singular ability to *introduce* the Torah to the world — to take something wholly superterrestrial and bring it down to Earth. Yehoshua's role, on the other hand, was to *translate* the Torah of Moshe in such a way that its teachings could be inculcated and its precepts applied by mortal beings leading a natural, post-*midbar* existence. In essence, Yehoshua's role was to reflect the "sunlight" of Moshe in a way that would illuminate his and all future generations.

Even Yehoshua's dimmer "moonlight," however, possessed sufficient intensity to guide Bnei Yisrael for generations to come. Yehoshua's accomplishments — leading the conquest and division of Eretz Yisrael and actualizing the Torah of the Dor HaMidbar as the Torah of daily life in the holy land — were truly impressive. Rashi comments (24:30)[ii] that a picture of the sun was etched on Yehoshua's tombstone to commemorate his awesome feat of halting the sun in its path (10:12–14; see our comments on

---

3. Even though the era of the *Shoftim* was rife with challenges and instability and lacked the degree of spirituality present in Yehoshua's time (as described briefly below), *Chazal* seemingly understand that, overall, those years were relatively calm and prosperous.

Perakim 9–12 above).[4] And *Chazal* recount (*Yalkut Shimoni* #22) that Yehoshua "argued" with the sun.[iii] *Mishbetzos Zahav* (pp. 194, fn. 30) explains that the sun did not wish to be dominated by Yehoshua, whose strengths were reminiscent of those of the moon. But Yehoshua won that contest and forced the sun to stand still, as he ruled, to a degree, over the sun as well.

Mission Incomplete

YET YEHOSHUA'S INFLUENCE had its limits. Bnei Yisrael seemingly never respected Yehoshua to the extent that they should have. *Chazal* (*Rus Rabbah, Pesichasa* #2; see also *Shabbos* 105b; *Rashi* 24:30; *Rashi, Sefer Shoftim* 2:7) teach that the nation was remiss in eulogizing Yehoshua after his passing. Thinking that they could manage on their own, and not realizing that it had been their leader's influence and holiness that had invited their success, Bnei Yisrael occupied themselves with their land instead of mourning the loss of Yehoshua. In the words of the Midrash (*Rus Rabbah* ibid.):[iv]

> Their portion [of Eretz Yisrael] was too precious to them. [Bnei] Yisrael would occupy themselves with their work — this one toiled in his field, and this one in his vineyard... they were remiss in performing kindness for Yehoshua. And Hashem desired to cause the entire world to overwhelm its inhabitants.

R. Tzaddok HaKohen (*Pri Tzaddik: Bereishis, Ma'amar Kedushas Shabbos* #7, p. 20a, s.v. ובמתן)[v] adds that this shortcoming was manifest even during Yehoshua's lifetime. Rather than revering Yehoshua's character and mirroring his example (in Torah learning and all that follows), Bnei Yisrael focused excessively and obsessively

---

4. See *Tzitz Eliezer* (vol. 9 #44), who explains why it was permissible to erect such a monument.

on settling their new land. This lapse, explains R. Tzaddok, prevented Bnei Yisrael from maximizing their spiritual potential.

Moreover, the elders of the generation, remembering vividly Moshe's supremacy, had difficulty fully accepting and respecting Yehoshua, whose greatness could not match that of Moshe (see our notes to *Perakim* 1–4; *Bava Basra* 75a — "זקנים שבאותו הדור אמרו" וכו'; *Mishbetzos Zahav*, bottom of p. 326). *Chazal* write (*Yalkut Shimoni* #959, on *Mishlei* 21:20) that people even referred to Yehoshua as a fool![vi] They saw him as a "mere student" of Moshe; not as a giant in his own right. They overlooked the virtue of being a "student," of clinging to a mentor and imbibing his every thought and action (see R. Elimelech Gottlieb's *Pnei Melech, Bamidbar* pp. 255–256).

The inability of Bnei Yisrael to recognize their leader's greatness and to soak up Yehoshua's wisdom and sanctity — in the way that Yehoshua did with his mentor, Moshe — left them bereft of a clear successor to Yehoshua. No individual had been groomed for the task.[5] Moreover, without comprehending the vastness of their loss, it was exceedingly difficult for them to fill the void created by Yehoshua's passing (similar to that which nearly occurred with Moshe's passing; see our comments to *Perakim* 1–4).[6]

---

5. For alternative reasons why Yehoshua seemingly did not appoint a successor, see *Midrash Shmuel* (*Avos* 1:1, s.v. ומסרה ליהושע).

6. *Chazal* note (*Bereishis Rabbah* 98:21) that Yehoshua is referred to by the name "Shaul" (see *Divrei HaYamim I* 5:10). They explain: "Why does he (Ezra) refer to him (Yehoshua) as 'Shaul'? Because his (Yehoshua's) kingship was 'borrowed' (שאולה)." Shaul HaMelech, the Jewish people's first anointed king, was a moral and spiritual giant on a personal level, but he lacked some crucial leadership qualities; he therefore did not merit to be Bnei Yisrael's eternal king. (With Hashem's help, I hope to elaborate on this point in a future *sefer* on *Shmuel I*.) Similarly, Yehoshua was unable to establish an eternal dynasty. But this limitation was not necessarily indicative of Yehoshua's *personal* deficiencies. It may have been due to Bnei Yisrael's inability to recognize and latch on to his greatness, as described.

Bnei Yisrael's failure to properly respect and shadow their leader was coupled with the fact that Yehoshua himself was intrinsically not as great as Moshe.[7] As mentioned previously, *Chazal* (*Bava Basra* 75a) compare Moshe to the sun and Yehoshua to the moon. Only the sun has the ability to exude enough light to allow others (i.e., the moon) to shine; the moon does not have the ability to further reflect that light to brighten others (see *Meshech Chochmah, Devarim* 31:7).[8] *Chazal* further compare the *Shoftim* who followed Yehoshua to the stars (see *Mishbetzos Zahav, Sefer Shoftim*, bottom of p. 2; see also *Ben Yehoyada, Bava Basra* ibid.). Hence, the generations that followed Yehoshua had to generate their own, less radiant light (i.e., the glow of the stars), rather than rely solely upon the guidance they received from Yehoshua.

As implied by the passionate farewell speeches cited above, Yehoshua recognized that his people remained somewhat disconnected from him, and he appreciated how precarious Bnei Yisrael's loyalty to the Sinaitic legacy might become following his passing. In fact, *Chazal* remark (*Tanchuma, Mattos* #4; *Bamidbar Rabbah* 22:6; see *Rashi* 11:18) that Yehoshua tried to extend his own life by prolonging the conquest of Eretz Yisrael. Seemingly, Yehoshua wished to remain Bnei Yisrael's leader for as long as possible because he feared the spiritual decline that might befall his people once he was gone (see R. Chaim Ben-Senior's *Imrei Chein* pp. 142–3;[vii] R. Yitzchak Levi's *Parshiyos B'Sifrei HaNevi'im, Yehoshua* pp. 134–5[viii]).[9]

---

7. As noted, Yehoshua's limitations in comparison to Moshe were inevitable, for the Torah itself (*Devarim* 34:10) testifies that no person would or will ever attain the prophetic heights of Moshe.

8. For additional (and deeper) explication of the difference between Moshe as the "sun" and Yehoshua as the "moon," see the comments of R. Chaim Volozhiner (*Likkutei Ma'amarim* #15–16, printed in the back of *Nefesh HaChaim*).

9. *Chazal* (ibid.) write that Yehoshua was incorrect for trying to prolong the

And as Yehoshua feared, the period of the *Shoftim* that followed his passing was marked by confusion, weak leadership, and defiance of authority (see below). Had the Jews properly appreciated Yehoshua, they would have been able to fully assimilate his teachings and seamlessly create further "light" of their own. They would have both groomed and merited a leader similar to Yehoshua — one who could have led them directly toward the world's destiny and ultimate redemption. But Bnei Yisrael chose a variant path, and history therefore followed a more tortuous course.[10]

Close of an Era

TO UNDERSCORE THE historic significance of Yehoshua's death and the attendant end of an era, the *Navi* closes *Sefer Yehoshua* with the interment of Yosef's bones and the death and burial of Elazar HaKohen (24:32–3).

---

conquest of Eretz Yisrael. *Mitzvos* should be performed with alacrity, and Divine instruction should be taken and obeyed at face value. Yet Yehoshua certainly did not treat Hashem's commands flippantly; he must have believed his plan to be truly consistent with Hashem's will. Indeed, *Metzudos David* (*Sefer Shoftim* 2:21) writes that Yehoshua found the basis for his procrastination in the Torah itself (see *Shemos* 23:30). So pure were Yehoshua's intentions that a number of sources contend that Yehoshua never committed a bona fide sin during his entire life (see *Mishbetzos Zahav* pp. 208–9, 324–5; *Nachalas Shimon* vol. 2, p. 253).

10. In the broadest sense, mankind's task is to refine humanity and bring the world to its ultimate perfection, a condition that will characterize the eras of Mashiach and *Olam HaBa*. There are numerous paths that can lead the world to this state of perfection, some more circuitous than others. Mankind's sins have forced it to endure the whirlwinds of history and to trek along the arduous road along which humanity still travels today. Accordingly, Bnei Yisrael's shortcomings at this juncture diverted them toward a roundabout route to the final redemption. (For further elaboration on some of these ideas, see *Michtav Me'Eliyahu*, vol. 4, pp. 141–3. With Hashem's help, I hope to further expound upon these concepts in future publications on *Sefer Shoftim* and *Sefer Shmuel*.)

Yehoshua, the crown jewel of the tribe of Yosef, perpetuated and advanced Yosef's legacy.[11] Both Yosef and Yehoshua linked past greatness and future progression. Yosef served as the fundamental link between the forefathers (especially his father, Yaakov) and the future of Bnei Yisrael.[12] He spent his life unifying his brothers (i.e., the tribes of Israel) through their common heritage.[13] Likewise, Yehoshua linked the pristine Torah given by God to Moshe at Sinai and the Torah that would be studied, molded, and applied by mortal man for thousands of years to follow. Yosef and Yehoshua were each heir to an ever-lofty tradition (the heritage of the forefathers and the Torah given to Moshe, respectively), and each successfully shaped and sculpted that tradition in a way that could be bequeathed to and utilized by all future generations. With Yosef's burial and Yehoshua's death, Bnei Yisrael's direct link to the past waned.

The passing of Elazar similarly signified the termination of an immensely deep connection to holiness. Elazar personified the sanctity of his father, Aharon HaKohen (in the same way that Yehoshua embodied the perpetuation of Moshe's teachings and leadership; see *Mishbetzos Zahav*, bottom of p. 328). With

---

11. Yehoshua's accomplishments were foretold by Yaakov Avinu, who blessed Yosef's son (Ephraim) that Yehoshua (a descendant of Ephraim) would conquer Eretz Yisrael and disseminate Torah among his people (see *Rashi, Bereishis* 48:19, s.v. ואולם).

    The *Rema MiPano* (*Gilgulei Neshamos* #90; #116) adds that on a mystical level, Yehoshua was a *gilgul* (reincarnation) of Yosef!

12. See R. Gedalia Schorr *zt"l's Ohr Gedalyahu* (*Shemos* p. 60a) and R. Yehudah Eisenstein *shlita's Ohel Avos* (ch. 35) for numerous sources.

13. Regarding the disparate models of leadership represented by Yosef and Yehudah respectively and the unique mission of the tribe of Yosef throughout history, see R. Yochanan Zweig *shlita's Shiras Yam* (*Bereishis* pp. 308–320) and *Mi'Maamakim* (R. Alexander Mandelbaum, a student of R. Moshe Shapira *zt"l*; vol. 1 #31–32). I hope, with Hashem's help, to expound upon this distinction at length in a future *sefer* on *Sefer Shmuel*.

Elazar's passing, the nation's connection to Aharon's greatness faded.[14]

Absent their firm bond to Moshe and Aharon, the nation required a new leadership model. Subsequent leaders would not embody the unparalleled, all-encompassing spiritual heights of previous eras. No longer would a single individual exemplify all the myriad qualities of a perfect role model, nor would he represent or affect equally each member of the nation.[15] Instead, each leader would need to utilize his unique talents and inspire particular aspects of his people's manifold personalities.

Indeed, during the period of the *Shoftim*, the leadership model changed drastically. *Chazal* teach (see *Nachalas Shimon, Shoftim* 2:4) that over the centuries that followed Yehoshua, each tribe produced, in succession, a *Shofeit* (judge) to lead the nation. In accordance with the singularity of each tribe, each *Shofeit* possessed unique strengths and virtues through which he or she realized

---

14. The tragic consequence of losing great leaders of past generations is depicted poignantly (albeit describing a different point in history) by R. Aharon Feldman *shlita* (in an article entitled *"Gedolim* Books," printed in *The Jewish Observer*, Nov. 1994, p. 32):

> A *gadol* is someone who is an embodiment of all the values, the attitudes and the behavior that the Torah demands from a Jew... who has achieved a level of accomplishment in these areas far beyond that of almost all his contemporaries. The loss during the Holocaust of hundreds of such outstanding Torah figures meant for the surviving generations not merely a diminution in their collective level of Torah learning and piety, but also a diminution of their spiritual aspirations... A *gadol* is the ultimate model against which his generation measures itself. Without living examples, we are not inspired to use our full potential, and we unwittingly settle for mediocrity for ourselves, our children and our schools.

15. As noted above (see our comments on *Perakim* 1–4, particularly footnotes 6 and 13), Moshe and Yehoshua embodied, metaphysically, each and every member of the Jewish nation, and, as such, linked each individual to lofty spiritual planes.

distinct accomplishments and battled disparate evils.[16] Yet no individual *Shofeit* could exude the comprehensive grandeur that Bnei Yisrael witnessed in Moshe or Yehoshua. The *Shoftim* constituted an eclectic array of highly gifted leaders, who, in sequence, triumphed against a variety of challenges and glorified both God and Israel. But, the absence of an exceptional, unifying personality contributed to many setbacks — sin, civil war, and national confusion (see *Sefer Shoftim* 2:11–3:6 and ch. 17–21).[17]

Yet Hashem never forsakes His people. And the *mesorah* (Mosaic tradition) certainly was never broken. As the *mishnah* (*Avos* 1:1) famously attests, the elders received the Torah's teachings from Yehoshua and continued to pass them on to all subsequent generations. Although Bnei Yisrael did not merit a perfect successor to Yehoshua, they were blessed with many legendary personalities during the time of the *Shoftim*. And, as mentioned above, *Chazal* (*Tanna D'vei Eliyahu Rabbah*, ch. 17) characterize even the era of the *Shoftim*, with all its setbacks notwithstanding, as one of overall tranquility and plenty.

Accordingly, *Sefer Yehoshua* concludes with mention of Pinchas, a man of awesome stature whose guidance was indispensable to Bnei Yisrael throughout the years following Yehoshua's death (see *Mishbetzos Zahav*, bottom of p. 328;[ix] see also *Rashi, Sefer Shoftim*

---

16. I hope, God willing, to describe the various personalities of the different *Shoftim* and the evils against which they fought in a future *sefer* on *Sefer Shoftim*.

17. The nation would eventually demand yet another leadership model: a king, who is charged to represent God's sovereignty and glory through the external glamour of his monarchy (*Shmuel I, Perek* 8). The kingship model, too, was not as spiritually rich as were the reigns of Moshe and Yehoshua, but it best fit Bnei Yisrael's spiritual state at that point in history. See the comments of R. Dessler *zt"l* (*Michtav Me'Eliyahu*, vol. 4, pp. 141–3; see also vol. 2, p. 218), who describes the diminution of holiness that ensued when Bnei Yisrael abandoned the model represented by Moshe and Yehoshua and appointed a king. (I hope to elaborate on these points, God willing, in a future *sefer* on *Sefer Shoftim* and *Sefer Shmuel I*.)

2:1, 6:8). The reference to Pinchas links *Sefer Yehoshua* to *Sefer Shoftim*. It assures us that although Yehoshua is no longer, all subsequent eras were and forever will be connected to those great years that he reigned. Bnei Yisrael might sin or flounder, but they will certainly never fall. Even if by circuitous route, the Jewish nation will ultimately achieve its historic mission and fulfill its destiny.[18]

ENDNOTES

[i] בימי יהושע בן נון קיבלו עליהם ישראל עול מלכות שמים באהבה... שכרן של ישראל שקיבלו עליהן באותה השעה עול מלכות שמים באהבה, לפיכך האריך הקב"ה את פניו להן שלש מאות שנה בימי שפוט השופטים, ועשאן כתינוקות של בית רבן וכבנים על שולחן אביהם, וקבע להם ברכה שהיא מדה טובה לעולם.

[ii] שהעמידו תמונת החמה על קברו, לומר - זה הוא שהעמיד החמה.

[iii] בשעה שעמד יהושע בגבעון ובקש לשתק את החמה... אמר ליה השמש, אתה אומר לי דום? יש קטן פותח פיו ואומר לגדול הימנו דום? אני נבראתי ברביעי ואתה נבראת בששי... אמר ליה יהושע, בן חורין קטן שיש לו עבד זקן, אינו אומר לו שתוק? לא קנה אברהם אבינו השמים וכל מה שבתוכו?

[iv] היתה חלוקה חביבה עליהם יותר מדאי. והיו ישראל עוסקין במלאכתן - זה עוסק בשדהו, וזה עוסק בכרמו... נתגעשו מעשות גמילות חסד ליהושע. ובקש הקב"ה להרעיש את העולם כולו על יושביו.

[v] דור המדבר, שהם דורו של משה רבינו ע"ה שהוא פני חמה, הם שורש ועיקר מקבלי התורה שבכתב, שהוא אור החמה, שהלבנה מקבלת האורה ממנה. ופני יהושע כפני לבנה, הוא ראש למקבלי תורה שבעל פה. ודור באי הארץ, אלמלי זכו להיות יגיעים ועמלים בתורה, היתה אז ההתגלות דתורה שבעל פה לגמרי, שהיו משיגים כל מה שאפשר להשיג בעולם הזה, ולא היו צריכים לגלות כלל. אבל הם פנו כל אחד לזיתו ולכרמו, ואף הזקנים שאחריו כמו שאמרו ז"ל.

---

18. Even the leadership of Yosef (embodied by Yehoshua, as mentioned) eventually resurfaced when Yeravam ben Nevat (from the tribe of Ephraim) seceded from the commonwealth of Yehudah and formed *Malchus Yisrael*. And although Yeravam and his followers abused their power and lost their throne, the dynasty of Yosef will emerge yet again through the personality of Mashiach ben Yosef during the concluding stages of the ultimate Redemption (see *Michtav Me'Eliyahu* ibid.).

[vi] אוצר נחמד ושמן בנוה חכם — זה משה. וכסיל אדם יבלענו — זה יהושע, שלא היה בן תורה, והיו ישראל קורין אותו כסיל. ובשביל שהיה משרת משה, זכה לירושתו, שהיה מכבדו ופורס הסדין על הספסל ויושב תחת רגליו, לפיכך אמר הקב"ה איני מקפח שכרך.

[vii] הוא (יהושע) רצה לחיות עוד בעולם, לא למענו, אלא למען כלל ישראל. משה אומר בתורה (דברים לא:כט) 'כי ידעתי אחרי מותי כי השחת תשחיתון'... 'שכל זמן שיהושע חי היה נראה למשה כאלו הוא חי' (רש"י שם). אם כן, יהושע ידע בנבואה, או מפי משה, שכל זמן שהוא חי ישראל ילכו בדרך ה'. אם כן, מן הראוי לגרום שישאר חי כמה שיותר כדי שישראל ילכו בדרך ה' ולא יסטו מן הדרך. זאת ועוד, הקב"ה הבטיח (שמות כג:כט-ל), 'לא אגרשנו מפניך בשנה אחת, פן תהיה הארץ שממה ורבה עליך חית השדה. מעט מעט אגרשנו מפניך'. אם כן, טוב יהיה אם ילחם יהושע לאט לאט כדי שהארץ לא תשאר שממה. בכל זאת, חז"ל דקדקו ומצאו כי במעמקי לבבו של יהושע רצה לעכב את המלחמה כדי להרויח שנות חיים נוספות.

[viii] חשש איפוא יהושע מפני ירידת ישראל ממדרגתם הגבוהה בימיו, כאשר משה רבינו 'כאילו אינו חי כבר' כי גם תלמידיו החביב יסתלק מן העולם. הן הן המחשבות הרבות בלבו, להציל את ישראל, ולדחות, עד כמה שאפשר, את הסכנות האורבות להם במותו. ולכן חשב עצה זו, להאריך את ימי המלחמה, וכך גם להאריך את ימיו.

[ix] ראיתי בליקוטי רמח"ל ח"ד במאמר (כ"ד קישוטי כלה) וז"ל, ואלעזר בן אהרן וגו', הכח של משה ניתן ליהושע, והכח של אהרן באלעזר. אח"כ פנחס כלל את שניהם, ובכח זה תיקן את כלל ישראל, שהרי בשעה שמתו אלו השנים (אלעזר ויהושע), לא היה מי שיכל לתקן ישראל, אם לא היה הוא, וזהו שקברוהו בגבעת פנחס והוא בהר אפרים.

Glossary

The following glossary provides a partial explanation of some of the Hebrew and Aramaic (A.) words and phrases used in this book. The spellings and explanations reflect the way the specific word is used herein. Often, there are alternate spellings and meanings for the words.

ACHARON (pl. ACHARONIM): lit., "the last one(s)"; the later commentator(s), circa 1490 to the present.

AGGADETA (A.)/AGGADAH: the sections of Talmud and Biblical exegesis that address the philosophical, ethical, and historical — as opposed to the legal — elements of Torah. [For profound elucidation of this aspect of Torah, see R. Ahron Lopiansky *shlita*'s introduction to his book, *Time Pieces*.]

ASHKENAZIC: reference to the large population of Jews who are descendants of, and/or live according to the customs of, the Jewish community that resided in Western Germany and Northern France during the Middle Ages.

AVINU: lit., "our father"; a reference to one of our forefathers (Avraham, Yitzchak, Yaakov).

AVODAH ZARAH: worship of "strange" (false) deities.

B'IYUN: in-depth [Torah study], in close detail.

BARUCH HASHEM: blessed be God.

BEIS HAMIKDASH: the Holy Temple in Jerusalem, the holiest site on Earth.

BEKI'US: broad expertise; usually in reference to quick-paced study.

BEN TORAH: lit., "a son of Torah"; reference to a person who lives his life as an upstanding, religiously observant Jew.

BNEI NOACH: lit., "the sons of Noach"; reference to people who are not Jewish.

BNEI YISRAEL: lit., the "sons of Israel"; reference to the Jewish nation.

CHASSID (pl. CHASSIDIM): person(s) devoted to the service of God and ethical perfection; follower(s) of the teachings of the Baal Shem Tov; follower(s) of a Chassidic Rebbe.

CHAVRUSA (A.): a Torah study partner.

CHAZAL: the Hebrew acronym for *"Chachomeinu zichronam livrachah"* (our Sages of blessed memory); reference to the great Sages of the Mishnah and Talmud.

CHUMASH: (one of) the Five Books of Moses.

DAYAN: judge; often a reference to a Rabbinic judge.

DERASHAH: Rabbinic interpretation of *Tanach* founded upon literary allusions in the Biblical text.

DERECH HALIMUD: lit., "path of study"; methodology of Torah study.

DOR HAMIDBAR: the generation that sojourned through the desert en route to the Land of Israel after the Exodus from Egypt.

EISHES CHAYIL: lit., "woman of valor"; reference to a righteous woman.

ERETZ YISRAEL: the Land of Israel.

EVER HAYARDEN: lit., "the other side of the Jordan"; the eastern side of the Jordan River.

GEMARA: Talmud, usually the Babylonian Talmud, but may refer to the Jerusalem Talmud as well.

GER TOSHAV: a non-Jewish person who pledges to abide by particular laws; as an upstanding non-Jew, he is entitled to a number of benefits, including permission to reside in the Land of Israel.

HALACHAH (pl. HALACHOS): the entire body of Jewish law, which instructs all facets of life, including ritual, financial, social, and familial; specific law(s).

HAGAON/GAON: the genius/genius; often used as an esteemed title for a great Rabbi.

HAMELECH/MELECH: the king/king.

HANAVI: the prophet.

HASHEM: lit., "the Name"; referring to God.

HASKALAH: lit., "Enlightenment"; the European intellectual movement known as the "Jewish Enlightenment" (late eighteenth to nineteenth centuries), aimed at "modernizing" Jewish thought; it drew numerous Torah-observant Jews away from their ancient religious beliefs.

KAREIS: lit., "cut off"; a Divine punishment for violating certain prohibitions — manifest as premature death, bereavement of one's children, and/or the forfeiture of spiritual life after death (see *Tosafos, Yevamos* 2a s.v. אשת; *Rambam, Hilchos Teshuvah* 8:1; *Maharatz Chayes, Yevamos* ad loc.).

KESUVIM: Writings.

KLAL YISRAEL: lit., the "entirety of Israel"; reference to the Jewish nation.

KOHEN (pl. KOHANIM): descendant(s) of Aharon, who is afforded various roles of distinction, such as the right (and obligation) to serve as priest(s) in the Temple.

KOLLEL: group of scholars who dedicate their time to Torah study.

KORBAN: an offering or sacrifice, usually brought in the Temple.

KORBAN PESACH: sacrificial offering of the Pascal lamb.

LEVI (pl. LEVI'IM): descendant(s) of the tribe of Levi, who, like a *Kohen*, is of an elite class and merited the right (and obligation) to serve in various roles in the Temple.

MANN: "manna"; the spiritual and physical food that God provided the Jewish people in the desert.

MASHGIACH: spiritual leader.

MASHIACH: the Messiah.

MEGILLAH (pl. MEGILLOS): scroll(s); often a reference to (one of) the five books of *Kesuvim: Shir HaShirim, Rus, Eichah, Koheles, Esther.*

MIDBAR: lit., desert; often a reference to the desert that the Jewish people traversed from Egypt en route to Israel.

MISHKAN: the Tabernacle erected in the desert, designated for sacrificial offerings and service of God.

MISHNAH: one of the earliest compendiums of the Oral Torah; specific paragraphs of that compendium.

MITZVAH (pl. MITZVOS): commandment(s) of the Torah.

NACH: the Hebrew acronym for "*Nevi'im* and *Kesuvim*" (the Prophets and Writings). [For elucidation of the distinctions between *Nevi'im* and *Kesuvim*, see *Nachalas Shimon* (*Yehoshua*, pp. 23–30); *Machazeh Elyon* (3:2, 4); *Emes L'Yaakov* (*Al HaTorah*, Preface, p. 12, #7).]

NACHAS: the pride and joy one reaps from children, grandchildren, an accomplishment, etc.

NAVI: a prophet; sometimes a reference to a specific prophet and sometimes to one of the books of the Prophets.

NEVI'IM RISHONIM: lit., "the first prophets"; often a reference to the first four books of the Prophets: *Yehoshua, Shoftim, Shmuel,* and *Melachim* (see *Nachalas Shimon, Yeshayah,* vol. 1, ch. 1, fn. 15; see also *Machazeh Elyon* 1:4, pp. 38–40).

OLAM HABA: the World to Come, the Afterlife.

PARDES: the Hebrew acronym for *"peshat, remez, derash, sod"*; different levels of interpretation of the Torah, spanning from apparent meaning to highly exegetical.

PASUK (pl. PESUKIM): verse(s).

PEREK (pl. PERAKIM): chapter(s).

PESHAT: the simple, literal meaning of a word, verse, Talmudic passage, etc. (For further elaboration, see the introductory essay, A Few Words on *"Derech HaLimud"* When Studying *Tanach,* pp. 40–44.)

POSEK: a Rabbi qualified to deliver rulings in halachah; authority on Jewish law.

RABBEINU: lit., "our teacher"; a respectful title given to some leaders and great Rabbis.

RAV (pl. RABBANIM): Rabbi(s).

REBBE (pl. RABBEIM): Rabbinic teacher(s).

REBBE MUVHAK: Rabbinic teacher from whom one learned the (near) majority of his Torah knowledge.

RISHON (pl. RISHONIM): lit., "first one(s)"; often a reference to the early commentators who lived following the period of the *Geonim* until the *Acharonim,* circa 1060–1490 C.E.

ROSH YESHIVAH: Rabbinic head of a yeshivah.

SEFER (pl. SEFARIM): book(s); in this context, a reference to a sacred text or texts.

SEPHARDIC: reference to the large population of Jews who are descendants of, and/or live according to the customs of, the Jewish communities that resided mainly in Spain, Portugal, and Africa during the Middle Ages.

SHEIVET (pl. SHEVATIM): one of the twelve tribes of Israel who are named for and descend from Yaakov Avinu's twelve sons.

SHLITA: the Hebrew acronym for *"sheyichyeh l'orech yamim tovim arukim"* (may he live a good long life); a blessing often appended to the name of a Rabbinic leader or righteous individual.

SHOFEIT (pl. SHOFTIM): lit., judge(s); often a reference to the various leaders of the Jewish people between the eras of Yehoshua and Shmuel HaNavi.

TALMID CHACHOM (pl. TALMIDEI CHACHOMIM): Torah scholar(s).

TANACH: the Hebrew acronym for *"Torah, Nevi'im,* and *Kesuvim"* (the five books of the Torah, the Prophets, and the Writings).

TORAH SHE'BE'AL PEH: the Oral Torah, which, in contrast to the Written Torah, was transmitted orally from generation to generation; much was eventually recorded in the Mishnah, Gemara, and later books.

YAM SUF: the body of water that the Jewish people crossed miraculously after their redemption from Egypt; often translated as the Red Sea or Sea of Reeds (see R. Ari Zivotofsky's article: https://www.ou.org/torah/machshava/tzarich-iyun/tzarich_iyun_the_translation_of_yam_suf/).

YESHIVAH: Torah academy.

YIRAS SHAMAYIM: fear of Heaven.

YISRAEL: an additional name given to Yaakov Avinu (*Bereishis* 32:28); often a reference to the Jewish people (descendants of Yaakov/Yisrael).

ZT"L: the Hebrew acronym for *"zecher tzaddik livrachah"* (may the memory of the righteous be a blessing); used as a respectful appendage to the name of a deceased righteous individual. [See Maharal (*Gur Aryeh, Bereishis* 6:9), who explains why this term is used specifically for the deceased. See also R. Yisroel Reisman's *Pathways of the Prophets* (p. 421) for an amusing anecdote and for some sources that indicate that this term may be used for the living as well.]

לעלוי נשמות

החזן ר' **אברהם יהושע** ב"ר צבי אלעזר זייף ז"ל
Cantor Abraham Seif
נפטר י"ז ניסן תשס"ח

ואשתו יהודית מרים בת שלום ע"ה
Edith Miriam Seif
נפטרה כ"ג אב תשע"ו

האשה חנה שרה בת יחיאל זאב ע"ה
Chane Silverberg
נפטרה כ' שבט תשע"ג

האשה רחל סימא סייף ע"ה בת ר' **אברהם יהושע** זייף ז"ל
Mrs. Shelly Seiff
נפטרה שבת קודש כ' חשון תש"ס

ר' **ישראל אריה** ב"ר אברהם יהושע זייף ז"ל
Alan B. Seif

גולדה ע"ה בת ישראל אריה זייף ז"ל
Golda Seif
נפטרה י"ח שבט תשנ"א

הרב יוסף אריה ליב בן משה הלוי הבר זצ"ל
Rabbi Yossi Heber
נפטר עשרה בטבת תשמ"ח

Jack and Ethel Perlstein ז"ל

ת.נ.צ.ב.ה.

הונצחו ע"י
הרב צבי אלעזר וליבא דינה זייף ומשפחתם
Rabbi Howard & Dena Seif & Family

In honor of

Rabbi Rafi and Malki Stohl

for their dedication to
Torah learning and teaching.

Daniel and Alyssa Barzideh

In honor of

Rabbi Stohl

and all those whose
mission is to increase Torah
in our community and around the world.

**David and Amy Lasko
and family**

In honor of our dear brother,
brother-in-law, and uncle

Yaakov Tzvi Kelemer נ"י

who personifies what it means to have
a *lev tov* and inspires us with his
passion for Torah learning.

**Rivka and Norman Ginsparg
and family**

In honor of
our loving parents

**Sam and Arlene Lasko
Max and Beverly Rubinstein**

Jon and Ellen Lasko

In honor of

Rabbi Stohl's

amazing accomplishments,
which are just beginning.

Steven and Martine Newman

L'iluy nishmas

the *Kedoshim* of our family
who were lost in the *Shoah Hy"d*.
The heroism, *emunah*, and timeless Torah values
contained in this *sefer* are a fitting tribute to
their memories and their *neshamos*
who will live on forever.

Rabbi Adir and Hindi Posy

In honor and
appreciation of

Rabbi Raphael Stohl

for his commitment
and zeal to enlighten
our Torah learning in the
Hollywood community.

The Kogan Family

In honor of
אמנו מורתנו

Natalie Baitner

for always instilling
within us a love of
לימודי קודש and תנ״ך.

**Avi and Judy
Baitner**

In honor
of our children

משה אליהו
דניאלה טובה
אברהם מרדכי

**Jordan and Tammy
Ditchek**

לעילוי נשמת

אהרן בן ברוך
שמואל שמשון בן ישראל
אליעזר בן אברהם
מתתיהו משה בן שלמה

**Jonah and Estie
Mermelstein**